ADVANCE PRAISE FOR
FIRE IN EVERY DIRECTION

"In a time when it can feel like language has been stripped of meaning and words have lost all power, *Fire in Every Direction* arrives as an affirmation and a refusal of silence. Luminous, moving, and achingly beautiful, every page of this book is guided by Tareq Baconi's fierce intelligence and a tenderness that this world does not deserve. You do not read this book to repair your heart, you read this book to understand the fissures."

—Maaza Mengiste, author of *The Shadow King*

"Outstanding . . . I found the blend between the personal and political to be very cleverly achieved. A brilliant book."

—Raja Shehadeh, author of
We Could Have Been Friends, My Father and I

"A powerful memoir of queer and Palestinian reckoning. Tareq Baconi creates 'a gaze of our own' by bringing his open heart to a tough confrontation with histories both intimate and diasporic. An important contribution to our many literatures."

—Sarah Schulman, author of *Let the Record Show* and
The Fantasy and Necessity of Solidarity

"In this moving and generous memoir, Tareq Baconi refuses to separate the story of sexual identity from the story of political commitment, and in so doing models a way to see our personal struggles as intertwined with our collective ones. *Fire in Every Direction* is a beautiful account of one man's confrontation with the histories, silences, and desires—both communal and private—that have made him who he is."

—Isabella Hammad, author of *Enter Ghost* and
Recognizing the Stranger

"In *Fire in Every Direction*, we not only see how the oppression of a people has affected one Palestinian family but how oppression in all forms—colonialism, patriarchy, homophobia, to name a few—creates dishonesty and masks within all of us. Tareq Baconi offers us a love letter, a blueprint on how to craft a life that questions the present, dreaming a better future in the process. By reading this beautifully honest memoir, we can learn to shed what must be shed in order to regain an allegiance toward justice, toward freedom, toward a liberation for all. Baconi has shown me that revolutions begin in the self; I am forever changed after reading this book."

—Javier Zamora, author of *Solito*

"With passion, sincerity, and wit, Baconi writes about the world he grew up in, about a time and place long gone, revivified in these beautiful pages. Spending time with the real people in *Fire in Every Direction* is a delight. Read this book!"

—Rabih Alameddine, author of *Comforting Myths* and *An Unnecessary Woman*

"With eloquence, passion, and insight, Tareq Baconi weaves his personal story as a queer kid growing up in the refugee community in Jordan into the larger narrative of his family's dislocation and the Palestinian struggle. In so doing, he gives new meaning to the concept of liberation, personal and political. *Fire in Every Direction* is primarily a love story: about how one learns to overcome loss—of a homeland, of a beloved—due to the interventions of authorities, be they parents or conquerors. It is a deeply inspiring and absorbing read, especially in these times."

—Mark Gevisser, author of *The Pink Line*

ALSO BY TAREQ BACONI

Hamas Contained

FIRE IN EVERY DIRECTION

TAREQ BACONI

WASHINGTON
SQUARE PRESS

ATRIA

New York Amsterdam/Antwerp London
Toronto Sydney/Melbourne New Delhi

WASHINGTON SQUARE PRESS

ATRIA

An Imprint of Simon & Schuster, LLC
1230 Avenue of the Americas
New York, NY 10020

For more than 100 years, Simon & Schuster has championed authors and the stories they create. By respecting the copyright of an author's intellectual property, you enable Simon & Schuster and the author to continue publishing exceptional books for years to come. We thank you for supporting the author's copyright by purchasing an authorized edition of this book.

No amount of this book may be reproduced or stored in any format, nor may it be uploaded to any website, database, language-learning model, or other repository, retrieval, or artificial intelligence system without express permission. All rights reserved. Inquiries may be directed to Simon & Schuster, 1230 Avenue of the Americas, New York, NY 10020 or permissions@simonandschuster.com.

Copyright © 2025 by Tareq Baconi

All rights reserved, including the right to reproduce this book or portions thereof in any form whatsoever. For information, address Atria Books Subsidiary Rights Department, 1230 Avenue of the Americas, New York, NY 10020.

First Washington Square Press/Atria Books hardcover edition November 2025

WASHINGTON SQUARE PRESS / ATRIA BOOKS and colophon are registered trademarks of Simon & Schuster, LLC

Simon & Schuster strongly believes in freedom of expression and stands against censorship in all its forms. For more information, visit BooksBelong.com.

For information about special discounts for bulk purchases, please contact Simon & Schuster Special Sales at 1-866-506-1949 or business@simonandschuster.com.

The Simon & Schuster Speakers Bureau can bring authors to your live event. For more information or to book an event, contact the Simon & Schuster Speakers Bureau at 1-866-248-3049 or visit our website at www.simonspeakers.com.

Manufactured in the United States of America

1 3 5 7 9 10 8 6 4 2

The Library of Congress Cataloging-in-Publication Data has been applied for.

ISBN 978-1-6680-6856-4
ISBN 978-1-6680-6858-8 (ebook)

TO MAMA AND BABA

PROLOGUE

THE yellow box is worn, its corners collapsing. The green and blue paint stripes streaked across its sides have lost their brightness. The cardboard of its body has sagged, crushed under the weight of travel—Amman, London, Sydney, Beirut, Ramallah. Forced to hold more and more content over the years, its bottom threatens to give way. Its handles almost rip as I move the box to my desk here in London.

Lifting the lid releases childhood smells: sugary sweetness and perfumed paper. The inside of the cover has a scribbled note from high school friends who had gifted me the box, wishing me a meaningful graduation, not knowing that it would come to contain an archive I would visit only occasionally, but otherwise keep safely entombed.

Shortly after Ramzi's news reached me, the messenger oblivious to how her words landed, I retrieved the box. Dust had settled on its lid. I peer in. On top are Tata's diaries, my maternal grandmother, which I have only recently inherited. I set those aside, not yet ready to turn their pages. I sift through the rest of the content. There are scores of letters; cards received from friends and family; old journals and pads; notes written on torn pieces of paper by classmates who passed them along during class; and paraphernalia, including a pack of decades-old chewing gum, toilet rolls printed with bright red hearts and lips, stickers, Christmas ornaments, and, for some reason that is no longer known to me but which is frightfully prescient, surgical masks.

I pull up Ramzi's side of our correspondence. This stack, disentangled from the box and organized beside my laptop, includes a picture in an unaddressed white envelope. Two barely recognizable teenagers are perched on a ledge. Their backpacks and sweaters are in a heap next to them. The two boys are on the final landing of the three sets of stairs leading from the classrooms to the main playground. The one on the right, I know, was posing not for the picture but for two other students coming down the stairs. The blue railings snaking alongside the stairs are, I recall vividly, behind the photographer, whose identity I have forgotten. The basketball courts and football pitches are filled with screaming children on the other side of the landing. Looking at the boy on the left, I remember how dry his skin felt in that morning sun, how the medication he had been taking for his acne made him dehydrated and itchy. Even though those kids' most guarded thoughts are still a part of me, there is a vast distance between us, a whole life lived.

I kept Ramzi's notes from the very beginning—not just his, everyone's, before I realized that I was keeping everyone's to avoid acknowledging that I wanted to keep only his. Everything he had given me, even before our correspondence had evolved into what it would become—proper letters, pages long, stapled and enveloped. Those were all in the yellow box, alongside a smaller box that contains two cigarettes and a bullet. The blue ink on the cigarettes is still legible. One reads, *20.01.2000. Time: 3.45. Rules: 1. Smoking is a pleasure. 2. There is no way out of this country except through loving someone. Enjoy.* The second: *Fuck Davidoff and Marlboro. This cigarette is from my last packet.*

It was not. On my seventeenth birthday, a month later, there was another cigarette stuffed into the card I received. I slip the card out of the envelope and open it. The cigarette is almost flattened in the crease, but the writing on it remains clear and crisp. *Happy Birthday TB, it really is nice to have you by my side. Love you, but not a lot. R.* The bullet, if I remember correctly, is from a camping trip he had gone on with his father to north Jordan. I had refused to join, much to his frustration. *You want me to spend a whole day just with him; it will be lecture after lecture.* His complaints resonate in my mind. I sift through his other gifts. Chocolates, candy, photographs, cards, and skillfully drawn vulgar pornographic sketches: three-dicked aliens and multi-boobed creatures in twisted sexual positions.

In front of me is a trail, his side of the letters we wrote to each other as we fell in love. We wrote on anything we could find; yellow legal notepads or blank A4 sheets, pages torn out of notebooks or the backs of cigarette packets, whatever scraps were lying around our homes. We left them on each other's beds or in our backpacks whenever we couldn't meet, for whatever reason, and our conversations had to find other ways to meander. I am reminded that his letters were neat; the lines never sloped, even on unlined paper. His handwriting was tight and cursive, lines of English interspersed with a strange hybrid of Arabic—colloquial words written with the full diacritics of formal Arabic. At the bottom of the pile is the first note I got from him. It is little more than a hasty scrawl that I can barely decipher on the torn corner of what looks like a textbook—geography, maybe, or history—laminated paper that has browned with time.

Sometimes I would leave his place, walk back to mine, only to find a letter stuffed into my backpack. Those were the most precious, letters that held thoughts that bordered on confessions, ones that grew beyond the confines of any one exchange and instead contained words that could not be spoken. Text that he was depositing in my safekeeping. Words that were directed at me but were not necessarily *for* me, that made me a container for his musings, a human journal. Made me, also, his witness. Some letters were full of recrimination, calling me out or raging at my behavior from behind the safe distance of a delivered screed. He was nocturnal, I wasn't, and when he couldn't call me late at night, he would write, imagine a chat we might have had if I were awake, embody my response, find himself against my words, and then leave me that record.

I treasured his written trust then, and today, I am grateful for it. In front of me is a transcript of his earlier self, one he has most likely forgotten or discarded. An archived monologue, waiting to be excavated. My voice is absent, not yet reclaimed, not yet molded into the voice of the man I am today. With my side of that correspondence missing, and with very little recollection of what I might have written him more than two decades ago, his letters help me retrace my past, make sense of my present, starting in Amman.

I

1

WE lived in a stone house in al-Abdali, on the seam between East and West Amman, where my parents landed after fleeing the civil war in Lebanon, privileged enough to bypass the east's refugee camps but not yet sufficiently affluent to settle in the west. One Friday in May, after our customary chicken tikka lunch takeout, Baba turned in for his siesta and Laith and I helped Mama clear the table. Tata took Nadim, five years younger than me and then still a baby, and put him down for his nap.

"Every week the same routine," Mama grumbled. "We never do anything exciting. There's a whole world out there, and all he wants to do is sleep."

Her discontent gnawed at her, whether we were out in the world or not. Laith looked at me and shrugged, then cruelly sniggered as he pointed to the raised step at the top of the tight corridor leading from the sitting room into the kitchen, where I had one day tripped and broken my arm. I shoved him as we followed Mama, placing the dishes in the sink next to where she was furiously scrubbing. "Go get dressed, boys," she declared, as if announcing a long-planned excursion. "We're going to Jerash to see the ruins."

Laith had been begging for weeks to visit the film set where part of *Indiana Jones* was being shot. After Mama had made sure Tata would not mind staying in and watching Nadim, we left. We drove for almost an hour, north out of the city, through the hills surrounding Amman, and down to Jerash, the town nestled between the ruins of a long-lost Roman world and the ruins of ours, in the form of the largest Palestinian refugee camp in Jordan, which had sprouted right next to it. Majida al-Roumi was blasting from the radio and Mama was lost in thought. Laith and I were in the back seat, bursting with excitement over this unexpected adventure, putting our faces by the open windows as warm air gushed in. My tongue, stuck out, was dry as cardboard. We were driving on the overpass built above the entrance to the camp when Mama turned the volume down. "Look how they leave them to rot in this place," she said, pointing to the camp. "Just look."

Laith scooted over to my side as we both stared out the window. The buildings were haggard, brown and stained, unlike Amman's polished limestone, and the streets denser and more cramped than other parts of the city. But I was not sure why Mama appeared so aggrieved. The scene did not look much different from al-Abdali or Amman's downtown—generally chaotic and overcrowded. Laith must have thought the same. "What am I looking at?" he asked. "And who's 'they'?" I added, thinking that those people congregating in the markets that had sprung up around the mosque after Friday noon prayers looked like they were free to go anywhere they wanted. Mama glanced back at us in the rearview mirror and said nothing for a few minutes. "The big shits," she said, as she turned the volume back up. "Men with fat asses who think they know what they're doing." I giggled as Laith—five years older than me and thinking himself an adult—leaned over to the front seat and tapped Mama on the shoulder. "Mama," he whispered in her ear, "you can't say 'shit' in front of Tareq!"

That was the spring of my fifth or sixth birthday, days before Jerash's annual summer festival was set to begin. We arrived in that part of the afternoon reserved for slumber—when the midday sun had not yet cooled enough to entice anyone out of their homes, and those who had ventured out carried themselves lethargically. We entered the ancient city through the Arch of Hadrian and walked into the esplanade that led to the grand Oval Forum, an expanse which gave a sense of the vast scale of the once-thriving metropolis. Merchants were setting up their stalls around the perimeter of the central courtyard in preparation for the throngs who would descend come dusk and stay late into the night.

We crossed the forum and strolled along the corridor lined with Corinthian columns, all the way to the Temple of Artemis. The vanilla-colored boulders carpeting the floor were like an obstacle course, uneven and scattered. Apart from two or three sweaty tourists, with cameras dangling around their necks and sizable backpacks on their shoulders, we were the only people walking in the heat. The film set that Laith was after had been constructed on that main corridor, and here, more people, mostly foreigners, were milling about. Laith got swallowed up by the crowd. Mama and I stood close by to watch. Even though the energy was frenzied, not much appeared to be happening, and I lost what little interest I had, becoming distracted, restless, my mind fixating on the market stalls we would walk through on the way back, heaving, I anticipated, with mounds of toys.

The sun was low by the time we returned to the Oval Forum and reentered a space that had, in the short span of time we were on set, somehow morphed from an imposing, majestic Roman arena into a bustling market resembling the one we had driven by on the way to Jerash. The smell of chestnuts and roasted peanuts wafted through the air and mingled with the steam from tubs of boiling water cooking sweet corn. "Lemons, grapes, oranges, grapefruits!" Merchants were shouting, riffing off one another and adding to the din of the gathering crowds. "Kitchen supplies, cooking utensils, bargains to be had!" Stalls piled high with fresh fruit and vegetables from the surrounding valleys had been set up next to others with stacks of socks and underwear, spices, and kitchenware. Shoppers had begun congregating in the market, haggling as they walked through. Arabic pop songs blasted from speakers that DJs had hung on the intricately carved crowns of the columns, which had been lit in purple, blue, and yellow. The space had a carnival-like atmosphere and I knew, before she said anything, that Mama would be itching to leave within seconds.

"We should head back," she said, on cue. "Baba will be waking up soon." My eyes scanned the stalls. It was the sparkle that caught my attention. I pulled Mama aside and into an alley. Tucked between rows of merchandise, dolls had been hung from the iron metal bars holding up one shop front. They were much larger than normal, more figurines than dolls—almost half my size and dressed in the most grotesque outfits. Mounds and mounds of chiffon and sponge-like material had been stitched around their waists to create bell-curve gowns that fell as almost perfect circles around their legs. The dolls had round, painted faces and their eyes were large and maniacal. Glittering beads had been sewn onto the gowns and the dolls had tiaras attached, glue visible, to their heads. The fabrics were washed-out pastel colors: light green, pink, and blue.

I latched on to an orange-brown one, transfixed, barely registering Mama's halfhearted attempts to nudge me to move on. "Come, let's go. We need to head home. Baba will be asking for us." Her efforts were futile; within seconds, the doll and I had become inseparable, destined to be together. Mama shook her head and turned to the vendor, an elderly man who offered an amused smile and a shrug of his shoulders. Defeated, she made the payment and walked away from the stall, with me and Laith in tow. I held on to my precious companion, her small, plastic hand in mine, fretting that her outfit might be crushed by the crowd. We made our way out of the market toward the North Amphitheater, where the stage was being set for an opera. Before walking to our car, we sat on one of the bottom steps for a brief rest. I made sure my doll had a comfortable position on the hard stone next to me and glanced up with satisfaction. The look Mama and Laith gave me was one I would become intimately familiar with. It was a look not unsettling enough to upset me, yet not so innocuous as to be forgotten either.

2

AL-ABDALI was our city within the city. Tata's friend from Haifa, Jalileh, had fortuitously become her neighbor in Beirut after the 1948 Nakba, and then again came to live a few minutes away after both had relocated to Amman. "This is another slice of Palestine," they kept saying to each other, as all around them and scattered throughout Amman were friends neither had seen since the Nakba. Family name after family name they rattled off to each other, guessing which town or village they had been supplanted from before settling in Jordan, decades prior to our arrival. "Ah, Masri," they would say. "The Nablus branch or the Jaffa branch?" "Yes, yes, Haddad, they're from Safad. They're Christian, right?" "Shehadeh, aren't they from Jaffa?"

Before I started going to school with Laith, and before Nadim was born, Tata would take me every morning to a nursery down the road, run by an American woman named Suzy, who had big blond hair and who had made Amman her home. The first day she dropped me off, Tata clung to me, unable to let go; Suzy had to prise me out of her hug. Her sadness at no longer having me as a toddler bound to her waist—"I feel empty," she kept telling Mama—soon gave way to routine. She would amble down the road in the early afternoon to pick me up, waving at neighbors as she went along, catching up with him and gossiping with her. A twenty-minute stroll would take an hour, and often involved being called into someone's home for a coffee or another person's garden for pruning advice.

One of my earliest memories was running out of the sandbox that had been placed in the nursery's backyard, under huge trees that filled the sand with sticky cones and dried pine needles, and into Tata's arms. That was the sandbox where one morning I shoved pebbles so far up my nose—to impress Maya, who was in the sandbox with me—they had to take me to the emergency room to pull them out. Tata picked me up every day, often alongside Maya's grandmother, and the two would chatter behind us as they pushed our prams back home. Tata would then put me in front of the TV while she finished preparing lunch, and I would watch dubbed Asian cartoons like *Sayida Mil'aqa*, the fantastical housewife with whom I was obsessed (*she could shrink herself to the size of a thumb and travel the world on her teaspoon!*), until Mama, Baba, and Laith came back.

I spent my first decade in that stone house. Memories crowd my mind when I conjure that world, before Ramzi and I met. The bloody knee I got running around our garden; breaking my front teeth as Laith chased me, pretending to be a vampire while Mama mopped the balcony; our conservative neighbor calling Mama to complain that Laith was playing basketball topless in the street, in eighty-five-degree weather—"He's making my daughter think impure thoughts," the neighbor had complained. "Good for her," answered Mama, hanging up. Other memories—inherited, excavated—also rush in. Memories that frighten me with their malleability, their unreliability. Their provenance. Most of what surfaces I brush aside, one after the other, until I am left with a few strands. These I order, curate to form a coherent whole, a singular narrative, one that might hold a spirit of resemblance to the truth.

◆ ◆ ◆

I am standing outside Tata's bedroom. She is awash in the sunlight seeping through the window above her bed, curled on her side, her hair a brilliant white in its rays. She has fallen asleep on top of the brown covers, her burgundy woolen shawl spread over her nightgown. Having lost all her possessions one time too many, she holds on to items, like that nightgown, which she wears to this day, more than thirty years later. It is just after lunch and the house is dead quiet. Mama and Baba are reading in their room down the corridor.

Tata is only half-asleep, attentive to the sounds around her. "I'm just resting my eyes," she would say, her eyelids shut. "I'm not sleeping." Not wanting to wake her, just in case, my toes land noiselessly on the cool floor. Her room is sparsely furnished, as if she has no need for worldly goods, with a cupboard and a chest of drawers that has three picture frames on it, lined up on a تطريز runner. One is of Mama and Baba on their wedding day. The other is of Khalo, Mama's only brother, with his Brazilian wife. The third is of Tata holding Laith, her first grandchild, when he was just a baby. She looks fashionable in the photograph, standing proudly in a brown polka-dot dress and large, white-framed sunglasses. On the bedside table next to where she is sleeping is her Bible—black, leather-bound, with *Holy Bible* sewn in golden Arabic letters across its cover. Numerous bookmarks protrude from its pages. The mattress sags under my weight as I climb on, snuggling into the space between her back and the wall.

"*Habibi*," she murmurs, "you've come to take a nap with me?"

What bliss. Safely tucked behind her, the knots in my stomach loosen. The sheets, toasty, warm my back. My eyes wander to the branches peeking toward the window, heavy with figs, and up to the shiny wooden crucifix above our heads. The taut muscles of the Jesus figure. The carved detail of his thorny crown. The burned wood around his stigmata wounds. That crucifix is one of the few items to have lived alongside Tata her entire life, watching over her as she slept. The story of its journey from her home in Jerusalem, how it came to hang in our home in Amman, remains only partially recounted.

My mind pieces together snippets of history, tales recalled and dramatized, clues dropped, sometimes inadvertently, over the course of a childhood. Lying next to Tata in bed, I ask questions that we only bring up in this space, prodding to get this detail or learn more about that, until I am met with silence, leaving me to imagine the rest.

3

يلى يلى—her father yelled from the bottom of the staircase one evening, "We have to leave, right now!"

1948. A shadow—the darkest one—cast over our lives in Amman. I pull Tata's diaries out of the yellow box. They are minimal. Barely anything is divulged, apart from her love for her God. Everything else documents basic events as they transpired, in a clinical and sober tone. A historian's archive rather than a record of a lived life. Her notes help me make sense of the tales that permeated our early years in Amman—unobtrusive, undemanding—like wallpaper on the back of our consciousness.

I see her, then a young woman, Eva, standing in her room, shaking, forced out of the stupor of the past few months. The spring afternoon was like every other that year. She had just come back home and was getting ready to help her mother in the kitchen. Her father, the local pastor, had left to go to church for the evening rituals. Everything ticked along as routinely as it always had, even as uncertainty clung to everyone. They were all stuck in a cycle, a relentless interrogation of a decision that had been made, one that had to be remade daily, incessantly.

Her father had decided they would not flee, and that was supposed to be the end of that. Even as more windows in the houses around them shuttered and front gates latched shut. Even as neighbors disappeared into the depths of the night without farewells or promises of reunion. Even as her girlfriend across the road vanished, as if her family had never occupied the two-floor villa on the corner, the one that had already acquired the forlorn look of deserted buildings. She knew her mother was worried, and that the firmer her father was, the more anxious her mother became. "I am the head of the parish, for God's sake!" he declared repeatedly. He was not going to leave his flock behind, no matter how rapidly it diminished. It had taken him two years—ever since they had relocated from Jerusalem to Haifa so he could assume this position—to gain the congregation's trust. What kind of message would he be sending his flock if he ran away?

"God works in mysterious ways," he assured them. If God wanted his family to be hurt, he reasoned, there would be a perfectly logical explanation for it. A divine purpose he could not possibly comprehend, let alone challenge. Even though Eva guessed he was as much trying to convince himself as the rest of the family, she was happy with that decision. She did not want to leave. Haifa had just started feeling like home, and she had finally grown to like her high school. Why go anywhere when she only had one year left before graduating?

Still, plans had to be made. Mundane contingencies despite all their heartfelt prayers. Necessary arrangements despite their rock-solid faith. Early in the year, her father had collected everyone's passports and papers and a few of their valuables and set those aside in a suitcase at the bottom of the stairs, where it rested that morning. In the beginning, Eva did not like looking at the suitcase as she made her way up and down the stairs. It was a reminder, even if subtle, of the times they were living in. But gradually, she had stopped noticing it. The suitcase blended in with the furniture of the house, its violence domesticated. Meanwhile, days unfolded smoothly.

Until spring came round, that is, when the news trickled in with even more urgency from all over Palestine. People whispered on street corners and in cafés around Haifa. The Zionists had mobilized. They were armed and vicious and determined, going from village to village, town to town, killing and raping. Thousands of Palestinians were fleeing. Entire villages were being burned and destroyed. At first, even this failed to puncture Eva's days. The snippets of nightmarish tales she heard were oddly out of place under the shadow of Mount Carmel, where, every morning, she left her house behind the Italian hospital near the port and walked the half hour to school. Down the boulevard that led to Wadi al-Nisnas and up the slight incline at the foot of the mountain toward the International Petroleum Company. Maybe she was immune to the tension consuming the adults. Maybe she was unable to live the words hanging in the air around her. But in the breeze of Haifa's spring, things seemed ordinary.

Regardless of the reason that made her denial so firm, it faltered all the same in the face of Deir Yassin. April 9, 1948—a date frozen in time, tightening its grip on our memory the further back in history it falls. A tranquil village, casually reclining against the hills surrounding the holiest of cities—her family's city, still her city—made to witness such gore. After Deir Yassin, the silence in her mind shattered. How could it not? The stories she heard were horrific, rumors swirling around: Boys and girls were paraded and lined up before being shot in front of their parents. A pregnant Palestinian woman had had her stomach sliced open by a Zionist terrorist, the fetus smashed. Grandparents were mocked and beaten to death by militias roaming the streets. The Zionists had wanted a gruesome spectacle, an example to others, people around her were saying.

That night, after news of the massacre reached them, her father turned off the radio in the kitchen and gathered them in the sitting room to pray. Eva stood between her brother and sister, and the five of them held hands. Her father led the prayer, the same one, he told them, that he would recount to his congregation that Sunday. "In these uncertain times," he said, "we need to put our faith in powers that are greater than us. Our Lord sent His beloved son, His only son, to be tortured and killed for our sins. Such is His love for us humans. Would that same Lord forsake us? It is at times like these, when earthly horrors come up against divine faith that we believers are tested the most. We need to look beyond our fears and anxieties. We need to lay our burdens at His feet, for they are too great for us to bear. 'Come to me, all you who are weary and burdened, and I will give you rest'—Matthew 11:28." Her brother squeezed her hand, comforting her. She had been raised a believer, and she trusted in an otherworldly goodness that would protect her family. Barely a couple of weeks later, as she was in her room, she heard the front door shut and knew her father was going to church.

He walked out of the house and turned left toward the city center. Before he had reached Haifa's main boulevard, the one that separated their neighborhood from the much livelier and more crowded Wadi al-Nisnas, he saw the barricades. The Zionists had arrived. They were erecting barriers across the streets and people were being turned back. There was no longer any access to the city center. Seeing the barriers drew his attention to something else: the sounds of shots descending from the Carmel mountaintop. He had been lost in his own thoughts, oblivious to those noises, thinking them construction sounds or the grunts of the city. Now that he heard them, while looking at this scene in front of him, they sounded ominous.

The feeling of physical confinement hit him with a force that left him suspended, unable to put one foot in front of the other. His mind, which until then had been whirring with messages of faith and conviction, grew still. He was not yet ready to admit what he understood, somewhere in his heart, to be true. Before that knowledge could sink in, before it could be considered and studied, before an informed decision could be made, instinct took over, and regret, where barely a few seconds earlier there had been certainty. *Was it too late? Had he left them here for too long? What would they do to his beautiful daughters? His son?* He rushed back minutes after leaving and slammed through the front door and into the house. Distraught, he shouted about Haifa being barricaded.

"The port," he yelled. "The port is the only way out."

The fear that had permeated the neighborhood since Deir Yassin suddenly had a face. For all the wavering minds, like her father, the message those massacres sent became clear. The price for staying put was too high. Eva had never seen her father like that. The calm soul, the gentle leader of the parish, the steady patriarch of the family, had gone out the door and returned a few minutes later a primeval shadow of himself. It is a frightful sight to see loved ones reduced to their most basic selves.

"Pack up! Pack up! We're leaving! Quick!" he screamed, jolting Eva out of her shock and back up to her bedroom.

I see her hands tremble as she reaches for the Bible and the crucifix. Her most treasured items. The two objects that made her room in Haifa feel like the one she had left in Jerusalem. What else does one pack when confronted with such madness? Perhaps a week's worth of clothes. A light sweater as well, for the morning and evening chill. She would be back long before winter.

"*Yalla!* Hurry! We're leaving now!" my great-grandfather shouted from the front door, where he stood with the bag that had long been prepared. The bag now fulfilling its purpose.

She saw her sister and brother run past her room with a suitcase each, followed by her mother, who rushed in and pulled a few more clothes off the hooks and into Eva's suitcase before slamming it shut. She grabbed her hand without any kindness, Tata would recall years later. No kindness, just haste, she told me, as if that slight was more offensive than the loss of her home. Eva tried to steady herself against her mother's pull as she exited the house and paused in its jasmine-lined entrance. Just beyond the gate, people were rushing toward the waterfront, their faces contorted. She looked back as her father locked the door and put the keys in his pocket. *Oh good*, she thought, *he's shuttered the windows*.

In the crush, she lost her bearings, and before she knew it, she was huddled between her older brother and sister in a fisherman's boat. Her hair was chestnut brown then, curly and short, from the old pictures I have seen—now bookmarks in her Bible. Her hastily packed suitcase lay by her feet on the wet floor. She looked at all the boats bobbing in the waves around her, and her eyes wandered toward the shore, where the lights of home melted away and those of south Lebanon shimmered in the distance. Lights that were desperately needed and wholly unwanted. A shudder ran through her body as the boat finally docked, and she joined thousands of others spilling out. She started reciting Bible verses in her head, she told me, wishing she was anywhere but on that pier. She clutched her mother's hand after landing, her other holding on to the suitcase with the Bible and the crucifix, the same one that hung above my head as I dozed off behind her every afternoon in Amman.

4

THE Tatas in al-Abdali visited each other daily, going to this one's garden or that one's balcony. They are in our house today, sitting on our back porch, drinking Arabic coffee with cardamom and gossiping. Laith is with the neighborhood kids in the alley behind our house and Nadim is napping. Mama is sweeping sand off our patio for the umpteenth time. "This is the land of dust," she complains over and over. "It is like emptying the sea with a bucket." With the broom, Mama is as much sweeping sand as expunging the fortune that had landed her here, in this desert city, hilly and hot, nothing like her Mediterranean Beirut. "We would just go for a dip in the sea whenever we wanted," she would say, making her days sound like an endless summer. Instead, here she was, in a sleepy town, sweeping, cleaning, waiting for Baba to wake up. I run barefoot across the patio, the sand tickling my toes, and jump down into the garden, sinking my feet in the soil. I walk around, looking beneath the bushes and in the far corners, trying to find my tortoises.

The Friday before, we had joined neighbors and friends on the hour-long drive to the hills north of Amman, where we frequently picnicked in a wood that had somehow been dubbed the Scandinavian Forest—a name that failed to live up to its fjord-like aspirations. The convoy of cars left the highway and climbed up the hill, parking near the top, right under a big green sign that read, "Forest of the Martyr Wasfi al-Tal, established 1973." Ice chests, trays of food, argileh pipes, and barbecues all came out of the trunks and we each carried a load toward a clearing that was, in minutes, buzzing with activity.

Baba joined the men, pulling up one of the white plastic chairs we had brought with us into a semicircle. A few were lighting coals for the argileh, which my dad never smoked, preferring his cigarettes instead. An ice chest next to them was filled with Amstel beers, and Baba picked one up as he settled down. I clambered onto his knees. "You don't want to play football with the other kids?" he asked. I shook my head and burrowed against his body as he rested his arm around me. I hadn't seen him this relaxed in months. He turned on his portable radio, which was just beeping into the short news segment at the top of the hour. Baba raised the volume.

"يا زلمة," one of his friends said, "give us a rest from the news."

A chorus of nods and yeses followed from the small group. Baba chuckled.

"There's never a rest for people like us," he pushed back.

"ليش؟ Is something happening?" another chimed in, worried.

"No, no," Baba was quick to reassure him. "Nothing here, thankfully. But the intifada next door."

"It's incredible. Abu Ammar must be losing it in Tunis. Do you think anything will come of it?"

"I don't know," Baba added. "How long do these people think they can keep their boots on our necks without a peep from us?"

"They've kept it long enough. Our cousins are determined, *ya akhi*, they're not going to give this up. You think a kid with a stone is going to scare them?"

Baba raised his hands in a prayer gesture to the sky, a sign of helplessness or confusion.

"But they look like criminals in front of the world," he argued. "They can't hide the occupation anymore when they're mowing children down. The US won't put up with this."

"They've been mowing children down since '48," another responded. "Look at Beirut after we left."

The men fell quiet. As the news segment wound down, another person broke the silence, calling on his kid to bring nuts for them to snack on.

"How's work going with you?" the man next to us asked Baba, changing the topic.

"It's good. It's good," Baba answered. "Things are slow. This country, مش عارف, it just doesn't have what it takes. Maybe I'll explore the market in Lebanon once things calm down."

Baba had been working for a small company with a manager he detested, and one day, after an acrimonious exchange, he had quit in fury, taking along with him clients whose loyalty he had won. "It is now or never," Mama preached, encouraging him to start his own maritime business, which he had long wanted to do. "I can cover us for a while," she insisted, even though her secretarial salary was hardly enough. It was a gamble that could have gone either way, and the odds were not encouraging.

The men started talking about work, and I slid off Baba's knees to go get Mama, who was sitting around the plastic table with the other women. A floral polyester cover had been pulled over the top and numerous Tupperware containers spread out: fattoush, tabbouleh, hummus, muttabal, falafel, za'atar, labneh. They were skewering lamb cubes, pieces of chicken, and kofta, marinated the night before, and preparing them for the grill. I tugged at Mama's blouse.

"It's just not possible," one woman was saying, "all those troubles start when you choose to marry someone who is not from your background."

"God help the children," another added, shaking her head. "They should just stay together. Divorce is cruel on kids."

Others nodded in agreement.

"By the way," someone piped in, "sorry to change the subject entirely, but did you hear that the Royal Automobile Club is postponing its pool opening this year?"

Mama turned to me and winked. *Yalla*, she mouthed, and then turned to the women.

"Let me just go for a walk with Tareq," she announced. "He's restless."

"*Habibi*, why don't you go play football?" Mama's friend said, pointing the skewer in her hand at the boys who had fanned out into the clearing, lining rocks on either side of the expanse to mark the goal posts for their game. Girls skipped rope next to them. I shook my head.

"*Yalla*," Mama said. "I'll be right back."

She wiped her hands, mouthed a *thank you* to me, and looked back to make sure Baba was distracted. The trick was to get him sufficiently engrossed in one conversation or another so she could slip away without him noticing her absence. Baba was determined to act as if he were unable to function without her. "Rima!" he shouted as we packed for the picnic. "Can you make me a Nescafé?" All morning, his demands rang out, one after the other. "Rima, have you seen my sneakers?" "Rima, don't forget to pack my portable radio." "Rima! Rima! Rima!" Rima put up with this, even as she grumbled that all she wanted was peace and quiet. She spent her days seeking both, with growing frustration at her failure to secure either. Out in the woods, as Baba fell into the commotion around him, and as Laith and Nadim were swept up in the football game, she and I melted into the shrubbery. Away from Baba's incessant nagging and the dreariness of Amman's small talk. Away from the shrieks of children. Away from the tiresome need to explain my disinterest in football.

"Thank you for saving me," she whispered as we walked away from the clearing. "These women can talk. Talk and talk and talk, and God knows what they're saying. My head is already numb. I need to stretch my legs."

We walked deep into the wood, which wasn't very deep at all, and around the periphery. We walked without speaking, the ground crunchy under our feet. Birds flew down from the bare treetops to pick up twigs for their nests. The sun splashed pools of light on the ground. The air smelled woody and fragrant, doused in pine. Only the evergreen trees were still green. In some corners, we saw the small white flowers that Baba told me were called dog farts. Empty water bottles and cola cans were scattered here and there, next to the charred remains of bonfires. We walked down to the barbed wire set up around the forest and then alongside it. Mama sought quiet on those walks, and that was fine by me, because I was hunting.

From our first visit to the wood, I could spot the tortoises ambling about, their short, stumpy legs protruding outward, bending under the weight of their shells. Some hunts failed; others yielded trophies to bring home. Anxious tortoise shit in the trunk of our car was not an unusual outcome from our days in the Scandinavian Forest.

That afternoon, we found a small one.

"How did you even see it?" Mama asked me. I beamed with pride and shrugged.

"She's scared," Mama said. "You'll have to take good care of her, carry her gently."

I nodded. Lifting her up as we made our way to the cars. I put her in the box I had prepared that morning, hopeful that I would find a new member to add to the family in our backyard.

Back in our garden the following Friday, hours passed with me sitting alongside my adopted pets. There was Kitty, the neighborhood cat, and Bingo, the tiny Pekingese from across the street, who often wandered over when Kitty—much larger than him—was not around. Kitty and Bingo and I were happy to spend whole days outside. With them, I imagined roaming forests and being shrunk, down to thumb size, like *Sayida Mil'aqa*. A creature small and light enough to ride Kitty or Bingo—a tiny creature surrounded by giants. Maybe to find my own giant, to be his pet, carried around in his shirt or trousers pocket as we roamed the woods. I spent many waking hours looking for him, sizing up men, Baba's friends or strangers in the street, whose pockets appeared sturdy enough.

5

EACH night, Baba, Mama, and Tata congregated around the TV set to watch the eight o'clock news, waiting to hear snippets from Beirut that might affect loved ones who had chosen to remain despite Lebanon's civil war: Baba's parents, Tata's brother, sister, and sister-in-law. There was often a communications blackout around Beirut, and when calls did go through, the best anyone could hope for was a garbled exchange of pleasantries against erratic static. The conversations were neither substantive nor fulfilling, but they nonetheless offered proof of life, and a temporary salve until the next round.

Normally, nothing on the evening news came as a surprise to any of them because Baba had his portable radio alongside him wherever he went, broadcasting updates from what was then Amman's only English radio channel, 96.3 FM, to everyone within earshot, every hour on the hour. And because he read Jordan's three main newspapers—الدستور, الرأي, and *Jordan Times*—daily, page by page. This fact did not stop them from sitting in front of the screen with fried nerves, as Tata said, every night.

Mama, Baba, and Tata had escaped Beirut along separate routes in 1976, a year after the war began. But that is not how Tata answers me when I ask when they fled. "We left after Tal al-Zaatar but before Sabra and Shatila," she would say. A timeline etched in massacres. Just as Deir Yassin in Palestine almost three decades prior had foreshadowed what might happen if Tata's parents stayed in Haifa, the slaughter of Palestinian refugees in the Tal al-Zaatar camp was enough to force the three of them to leave for Amman. Then came the months and years that fried their nerves, as they watched their country descend into a gruesome war.

Baba's parents, who had stayed behind, had internalized an altogether different lesson from the Nakba: It is better to die in one's home than in exile. It was a lesson that was incomplete. When his father did die of a stroke, in a besieged city that Baba could not get to, leaving his mother grief-stricken and alone under heavy bombardment, the full truth dawned on them: Neither exile nor home could ever offer shelter from heartbreak or the senseless violence of war.

◆ ◆ ◆

I was too young to have witnessed this myself; I was only two in 1985. The entry in Tata's diary, dated August 20 of that year, notes that she had heard *deeply upsetting news on TV*. I assemble the rest of the scene with recycled anecdotes, which is easy to do, because that evening has become the stuff of family folklore.

A hot August in Amman and a burning Beirut. The war had taken a bad turn. The initial fighting between Palestinians and Muslims on the one hand, and right-wing Christian Phalangists on the other, had given way over the course of a decade to ever-expanding violence between Lebanon's numerous sects and to Syria's involvement. Car bombs were once again exploding all over the city, and efforts to achieve a truce between the warring factions were faltering. The week before, leaders of the fighting militias had met in Damascus to try to carve out some kind of agreement, to no effect. Their failure tipped the city into another round of bloodletting. Baba is glued to the TV for the 10 p.m. segment alongside Tata, who is dressed in her light-blue nightgown. Laith and I have gone to bed and Mama is preparing a late-night snack for Baba in the kitchen. The news anchor is recounting the events of the day. A car bomb had exploded in a Christian district in East Beirut—"That's Hazmieh," Tata had exclaimed. "That's where Daoud lives!"—and the militias were exchanging missile fire from their bases over residential towers. Some apartment blocks were badly damaged by errant missiles, the anchor noted, as they cut to a picture of a burning building.

Tata leans forward, closer to the TV. She squints. A fire is billowing on an old roof, which is dotted with water tanks and laundry lines that have white bedsheets hanging from them, smudged with soot from the smoke. Suddenly, Tata is on her feet shrieking. "Daoud! Daoud! Leila! Leila!" she screams, pointing at the TV. Baba is looking at her like she is a madwoman as Mama rushes in from the kitchen, wiping her hands on a towel. Tata looks at Mama while shaking her finger at the screen. "That's them, that's them," she shrieks as she watches her brother and sister-in-law trying to douse the flames, dressed in their pajamas and night slippers, Leila's white hair done up in a nest of curlers, strands coming undone. The TV returns to the news anchor as Tata slumps back on the sofa, sobbing. Mama comes over and sits beside her, trying to comfort her. "Well," Mama says, holding her, "you keep complaining that you haven't seen them in a while. Here they are. They look well." Tata's sobs give way to a giggle as she smacks Mama's knee.

6

دايمة—Baba says one day after lunch, before he heads into the bedroom for his siesta, the stack of newspapers folded under his armpit. These he will obsessively read, cover to cover, before napping.

Khalo gets up from the dining table and sprawls out on the couch, his lanky frame and long limbs extending out across the living room space. Mama and Tata clear the dishes while my brothers and I gravitate toward our uncle, planting ourselves around him, taken by this familiar stranger in our midst.

Khalo is visiting from São Paulo, where he lives. About once a year, he comes to Amman to be waited upon as the golden boy of the family. From the moment he was nestled in Tata's arms in Beirut, barely two years after Haifa, her life had become tethered to his happiness. Khalo and Mama grew up in lockstep, eighteen months apart, but they could not have been more different. He struggled in school, so much so that Tata and Jiddo, my grandfather, worried he might not graduate. They fretted over his performance while Mama, who sailed through and excelled at every level, required very little attention. Come high school, a difficult decision had to be made. Choosing one of their two children to send abroad, Tata and Jiddo decided to pool their meager savings and enroll Khalo at university in Brighton. *The English will whip him into shape,* they reasoned, *and Rima is better equipped to hustle her way at university in Beirut.* This Rima would do while looking after them. It was an investment in Khalo that never quite paid off, but that mattered very little. For Tata, Khalo's subsequent mediocrity was the product of an amalgamation of bad luck, uncontrollable events, and the trials of the Lord. Despite doing a whole lot of wrong, Tata's firstborn, this middle-aged, balding man chain-smoking in our sitting room, could do no wrong.

"القرد في عين امه غزال" Mama mutters under her breath. "The monkey is a gazelle in its mother's eyes."

Khalo looks at her with a knowing glance and chuckles, secure in his preferred status. To Mama's chagrin, my brothers and I are also taken with this monkey.

"Do you boys want to play He-Man today or Transformers?" For his three adoring fans, Khalo is an adult-sized person who knows all the characters we've struggled to get Mama and Baba even remotely interested in.

"Transformers," Laith immediately answers. "I want to be Optimus Prime!" he says as he jumps up and down next to Khalo.

"Optimus Prime! Are you old enough to be the leader of the gang?"

"Yes! I am, Khalo, I am!" Laith pleads.

"Fine," Khalo says, "Tareq, you can be Bumblebee, and Nadim, you're Jazz."

We all nod enthusiastically, our eyes fixed on him in anticipation. Khalo takes a deep breath, theatrically reaches over to his packet, lights a Marlboro Red cigarette, ponders, and then leans back. He crosses his hairy legs, which are poking out from under his shorts, and balances the ashtray on his belly. Between puffs, he strokes the countable gray hairs he has remaining on the crown of his head and begins. In his suspenseful tales, Marvel action heroes mix with Disney characters, and ever-meandering plots keep us frozen in our spots, snuggled around his limbs until Mama, having lost her patience, shoos us away to finish our homework. That day, Laith and Nadim scurry off to our bedroom. I stay put in the nook of Khalo's armpit despite Mama's protestations. He looks at me quizzically.

"You have no homework to do?"

I shake my head.

"حبيب خالو انت" he chuckles, pulling at my cheeks. "Want to take a nap with me instead?"

I nod. Khalo draws sharply on his cigarette, a final drag, and puts it out on the ashtray hanging ever more precariously on the side of his belly. He gets up, tipping me over into the space he has just vacated.

Khalo is staying in Tata's room, where I normally take my naps. I trail after him, amazed that he has to bend to pass through doorframes. I scramble to keep up and follow him into the room. He shuts the door behind me as I climb onto the brown covers of Tata's bed and lie down, sleepy, my eyes gravitating to the crucifix, then back to Khalo. He takes off his watch by the dressing cabinet and places it, face up, next to the picture frames. He comes to the side of the bed and begins shedding his clothes, down to his white boxer shorts, saying very little to me, if anything at all. He is pretending I am not there. I am living the same pretense. A voyeur, working hard to keep my eyes open, watching intently his every move. His hairy belly hangs over the waistband of his boxers. My eyes follow him to the window, where he pulls down the shutters, plunging the room into a darkness that can only be had when it is daylight outside. Faint rays of light seep through, painting beams across the sheets and my body, and down onto the floor. Khalo comes to bed and slides under the covers. Without a word, he begins dozing off. His indifference to my presence makes the atmosphere captivating. Sacred, even.

I listen to his breathing. There is a subtle snore at the end of every inhale, like a gurgle or a small car's engine. Or maybe it sounds like Bumblebee's engine. *Tomorrow*, I think to myself, *I want to ask Khalo to play Sayida Mil'aqa with us. Maybe, maybe, I can finally have my giant.* Khalo's breath is rhythmic, steady. I lift the covers and slide under, taking off the T-shirt I am wearing. I press myself against Khalo's body and feel his warmth on my skin. The hairs on his torso tickle my smooth chest. His unusually long arms wrap around me easily, dwarfing me. His breath mingles with mine as the smell of cigarettes floods my nostrils. My hands roam his chest, finding his nipples. Next to my little fingers, they are gigantic, round and plump and very pink, surrounded by dark hair. His eyes remain shut. *I am lucky that Khalo has no kids, and that his wife has not traveled with him. I want to be the only one here.* I sneak up even closer. His body yields.

"Do you want to be my pillow today?" he mumbles drowsily, not once opening his eyes. "You can get between my legs if you want."

An electric current shoots through my body, arching my spine. It is hard to breathe. My mind has conjured what I wanted him to say. I flip over and dive under the covers toward his feet. Khalo dutifully opens his legs. I put my head between his thighs, with my feet up against his chin. He closes his legs on either side of my head and I snuggle closer, burrowing my face into his boxers, feeling the cotton fabric against my cheeks. I am cut off from the world, existing in my own haven. His thighs press against my ears, muffling all sound. It is pitch dark, and I feel nothing other than his breath on my toes. I inhale into the space between his legs. It is musky and humid, with my breath and his smell. I lie awake, reveling in the sensations washing over me. My own giant next to me in bed, offering an entire universe to explore. A universe I will return to, time and time again, in a game we call *pillows* throughout those months.

Khalo is asleep, I can tell. His body relaxes, giving way as his full weight rests on me, his thighs crushing my head. I do not know what to do with my hands, so I clasp them behind my back as I squeeze in tighter, breathing in.

7

JALILEH, Tata's friend who lived down the road from us in al-Abdali, was older than Tata but had a younger spirit, carrying her years with giggles and infectious energy. Her hair was pure white, and her face little more than puddles of wrinkles gathered around her tiny eyes. When she laughed, which was often, her eyes disappeared into layers of skin and her false teeth wobbled, threatening to pop out. She was tiny, almost my size as a kid, with a hunched back that made her look even smaller than she really was—small and energetic enough for me to pretend she was *my* friend, not Tata's.

Whenever we visited, every couple of weeks or so, Jalileh would greet us at the door with a bowl of white and pink sugar-covered chickpeas, to my delight, and usher us into the flat where she lived by herself. Tea would have been laid out on the table as I stepped into a tradition that the two of them had sustained for years, since the heady days of prewar Beirut. Sinking into the overstuffed sofa cushions between them, I watched a repeat of a movie I had seen countless times.

"I couldn't believe it," Jalileh squealed. "Eva, he recited the whole alphabet in English without any help! He was three."

She leaned in to pull on my ever-elasticized cheeks and pat me on the head. Tata nodded, no longer bothering to feign surprise at the heavily embellished story we had been hearing since I was three and practicing my alphabets with the two of them.

"I was telling our neighbor the other day, and he couldn't believe it either. Eva, he was three!" Jalileh poured the tea and giggled some more. "He's a genius, Eva. Your grandson, a genius."

There was the customary roundup of friends and family, checking off illnesses, deaths, and scandals. It was less a conversation and more a monologue delivered by Jalileh at extraordinary speed. As Tata sipped her tea, nodding and shaking her head at the right junctures, I tried to figure out how Jalileh breathed between the words tumbling out of her mouth. Mama said Jalileh's incessant ramblings gave her migraines, so she never came along. I could not resist the stories and insisted I join. Even to my childish senses, the significance of those afternoons—the hard-earned continuity amidst so much upheaval—was tangible. I thought myself lucky, chosen, to have been included, and readily played the role of spectator, preparing to take in all the wild stories they recounted from Lebanon, and before that, Palestine. My favorite was the one that unfailingly made Tata laugh.

"We were sitting having tea, just like this," Jalileh told me. "The war in Lebanon was still in its early months. We were on the plastic chairs in the kitchen in Hazmieh because the living room was too exposed with its windows. There were snipers in the opposite buildings, and we had learned not to sit too close to the glass. The kitchen had only one small window in the back. It was much safer."

I once interrupted Jalileh's flow to ask how Tata had made it over for tea during the war and under the gaze of snipers.

"Were people not meant to have tea for fifteen years?" she replied, shocked. "Anyway"—she flicked her hand, as if my question was an annoying fly she had to swat away—"we were having biscuits, and I was in the middle of a story, when out of nowhere, something crashed into the wall right behind me. A terrible, terrible noise. A missile!" she said, throwing her arms up in the air. "It flew into the kitchen and straight under my legs, knocking me right off my chair before bursting out through the other wall!"

Tata beamed with excitement and started chuckling as she set down the teacup that had been balancing on her lap. Her whole body was shaking as she tried to suppress her laughter. I knew what she was thinking. With tea and debris all over, and a stunned Jalileh on the floor, *Silence, finally! What else could get that woman to stop talking?* Tata's face showed that nothing could have quelled the joy she had felt at that stray missile shutting Jalileh up.

"حمدالله" they would both say after the laughter had settled. "He was watching over us."

There was much to watch over. At first, Tata refused to see that their adopted country was disintegrating. Lebanon had shown her kindness from the moment they had disembarked at the port. As Palestinians were forced into refugee camps, her family was spared the fate of joining them. Their Christianity had set them apart, in the eyes of their host government, from the uncivilized masses of Muslim refugees. Shortly after their arrival, they were granted Lebanese passports and citizenship, a path to a job and a flat. Two years after arriving in Beirut from Haifa, Tata and Jiddo, recently married, moved to a small apartment in Hazmieh, next to where Tata's siblings had settled.

The house where Mama was born and raised sat on an incline facing Tal al-Zaatar, a large camp whose refugees were among the first Nakba survivors to arrive in Lebanon. For Tata, they had been spared the camps because they believed in Jesus Christ. No matter that there would eventually be other Christians who were unable to get the same privileges, as the government soon limited its intake of even Christian refugees. "God works in mysterious ways," her father used to say in Haifa, and what was more proof of that than her family's fortune after their immense misfortune?

For Mama, the existence of Tal al-Zaatar was a scab that had to be picked at over and over again. Those were the camps they would have ended up in, *should* have ended up in. A fascistic policy was the only reason her life unfolded in the small flat down the road instead of in Tal al-Zaatar's ramshackle tin-roofed structures. This fact failed to puncture Tata's belief that Lebanon had offered them nothing but safety.

But as violence washed over Beirut, Tata's steadfast resolve began to crumble. One evening, early on in the war, knocks landed on their front door. It was close to ten at night and rounds of gunfire could be heard close by. Stuck in their routines, Tata and Mama had taken to turning on the evening news—to know what was happening, but more desperately, to compensate for the quiet in the house with Jiddo and Khalo both abroad. Jiddo was working in Saudi Arabia at the time, and Khalo had been sent to university. They had just finished their dinner and were cleaning dishes as the TV played in the background when the knocks startled them. The neighbors upstairs had left earlier in the week to go up to the mountains and wait out the skirmishes in the city. Tata had been offended that none had offered to take them along. They knew Jiddo and Khalo were away, leaving her and Rima vulnerable on their own. Mama had shrugged her mother's hurt off. "They probably blame us for what is happening in their country," she had said. Tata disliked it when Rima took that attitude. *Where were they supposed to go after Palestine—just vanish into thin air?* The knocks landed more heavily. The neighbors would not have returned yet. Without missing a beat, Tata pulled out the knife she had just dried and put away, the one she had used to slice onions barely a couple of hours previously, and pressed it into Mama's hand.

"Go hide behind the bedroom door," she whispered, "and don't come out until I call you."

Mama tried protesting, ready to shake the knife herself at any assailant, but something in Tata's voice melted her resolve. The knocks came again, harder, impatient, as Mama rushed to the bedroom.

"If you don't open this door, I'll break it down," a man's voice demanded.

His pounding left no doubt that he could. Tata walked to the door, drying her hands on the apron around her waist, and glanced back to make sure Mama had heeded her instructions. She crossed her face and mumbled a Hail Mary before taking down the latch and holding the door ajar. The gun was pointed straight at her heart. "My skin felt foreign to me," she once said while recounting this moment, as if she had flitted out of her body and were watching this middle-aged woman look down the barrel of a gun. The pounding of her heart became louder than the TV behind her. Her feet were glued to the floor even as her knees shook. She looked straight at the gunman. His balaclava was dark green, an olive color. He was much bigger than she was, his shoulders muscular and broad, taking up all the space in the doorway. The hall outside was unlit, and she could not see his eyes.

"Money. Give me whatever money and jewelry you have in the flat حجة," he said, in a low voice that, Tata would later tell me, barely covered his own nervousness.

He took a step forward, leading her into the flat as he closed the door behind him, never once lowering his gun. Her chest tightened. She was trapped. He was blocking the sole exit. Tata was the only thing standing between him and the bedroom where Mama was hiding. The TV glare landed on his covered face, and she saw that his eyes were brown.

"*Yalla*, where do you keep your savings?" he demanded, sounding rushed. "We don't need Palestinians like you in this neighborhood. I hear your daughter is trouble enough at university."

"I just knew it," Tata told me. "I knew that voice. I had heard it before. He was our neighbor from a few doors down, whom Rima and I waved to every morning as I went to work and she to university. Had he no shame, breaking into my home when he knew my husband wasn't there? All those shoulders and he needed a gun to attack two women in the middle of a night that rattled with gunfire? When I heard his voice again, and I realized who he was, I was empowered. God granted me strength. The Holy Spirit filled my chest. No, I told him, I will not give you any money. And then I said his name. Abu Issa. عيب عليك, Abu Issa, I said. *3eib*. Shame on you. I was praying in my mind, imploring the Lord, to get him to lower the gun. I was worried I would make him angrier. It is not easy for an Arab man to see a woman stand up to him like that. For an Arab man to have his strength and his might questioned. But God was watching over me. Go home to your wife and children, I told him, as I felt his resolve break. Go home and come back tomorrow after work. I'll welcome you as a guest. I'll serve you Arabic coffee and we can talk about how much you need. But put that gun down and get some manners."

"And you know what, Tareq?" she asked, turning to me decades later, sitting in her pink armchair, her hand resting gingerly in mine, her memories flowing softly, at odds with the fear they had once garnered. "He left."

8

WHEN Rima, not yet Mama, was at the all-girls Evangelical school in al-Hadath, the next neighborhood over from her home in Hazmieh, before she was old enough to grapple with the enormity of her history, she would often take a detour into Tal al-Zaatar on her way back. She ran around its alleys, playing football, and skipping rope. Although an outsider to the camp, she quickly became a part of its world, making friends with two girls and a boy: Mona, Lubna, and Abdullah. All three went to the UN schools administering to the needs of Palestinian refugees. Theirs were two divergent worlds, a fact the kids only took notice of when mocking Rima's school uniform. And not because hers was different, but because Rima's was, unlike their own crisp and ironed uniforms, without fail, rumpled and smudged, much to Tata's daily dismay.

With Mona's mother being the best cook, the four of them descended into her one-bedroom home for lunch often. "Where do you sneak off to eat every day?" Tata berated her, having cooked and waited for her to come back from school, and knowing full well the answer. "You should come back here for lunch. They barely have enough food to feed their own family in the camp." Be that as it may, there was enough to go around, and then some. Without fail, every time she went, Rima would leave laden with leftovers. "Take this," Mona's mother would say, "and give your mother a break from having to cook!" Rima gratefully took the food and, on her way back home with Mona, distributed it to others in the camp.

Whereas Mona's mother fed them, Rima's paltry wardrobe dressed them. On the cusp of starting high school, the four friends grew more adventurous, sneaking around the neighborhood and venturing into downtown Beirut. Rima and Mona, by then inseparable, spent hours in Rima's room, choosing outfits for their dates with this boy or that one, while Lubna and Abdullah fell in love, becoming school sweethearts on the path to marriage. Rummaging through Rima's closets, Mona turned her drab, baggy pants and shirts into sexy outfits for their nights out. "I work miracles," she gloated. "I just don't know what to do with you," she would add, pointing at Rima.

When Rima graduated from secondary school at the top of her class, there were no high schools for girls in the area. There was only the all-boys Evangelical School, also in al-Hadath, which offered the Lebanese Baccalaureate matriculation. That year, the school made an exception for three talented girls to join their cohort. Rima got the first spot, Mona the second. They were both, in double measure, excitable and anxious. "What will you wear?" Mona kept asking Rima, going through her closet over and over again in the lead-up to the beginning of the school year. "I'll wear the uniform we all have to wear," Rima answered. "I'm going there to study, not to meet silly boys." Mona looked at her, arched an eyebrow, and sighed. "All those boys will be wasted on you."

For once, Mona was not quite right.

◆ ◆ ◆

After landing in Lebanon as refugees from Haifa in April 1948, Baba's parents, also Christian, circumvented the camps but struggled to make ends meet. His mother, an office administrator, had to care for her eight younger siblings on her basic salary, and his father, a taxi driver, brought in just enough for his wife, son, and daughter to get by. With their limited means, Fadi and his sister, my aunt, qualified for a UN-administered school, alongside other poor refugees.

Fadi's father was an amateur diver on the side, a hobby he started in Haifa and sustained in Beirut. At the end of his shifts, he would pick Fadi up and drive him down from al-Hadath, where they lived, to the waterfront. Having spent all day in the car, he would get out, stretch his body, gulp in the sea air, and turn to the car's boot, where his scuba gear and fishing equipment were stuffed. Fadi would help him haul both to the edge of the water and assemble the heavy diving suit. His father would step in, secure the large glass bulb over his head, pull on thick rubber gloves, and waddle with this enormous weight into the water. Before submerging, he would flash Fadi a thumbs-up sign and disappear down to the seabed, looking for sea urchins. With his glove-clad hands, he could extract them from the cleavages in the rocks and stow them into the net pinned under his belt.

Sitting on the beach, waiting for his father, Fadi, then a young boy, would watch the shipping containers come into Beirut's main port further north and lose himself in thought, dreaming of one day owning a yacht and sailing onboard dressed in a white summer suit, smoking a cigar. His reverie would break only once the glass bulb of his father's helmet punctured the waves. Fadi would scramble over and take his father's equipment, as well as the net bulging with sea urchins. He would get to work, shucking a few open with a pocketknife while putting the rest away. As the sun set, they would drizzle the urchins with lemon and salt and slurp them while they waited for the gear to dry in the hot air.

It was at the UN school that Fadi aspired to change his circumstances, and by high school he managed to earn a scholarship to transfer to the all-boys Evangelical school in al-Hadath. In his second year, he and his cohort were both scandalized and intrigued by the three girls who had been admitted into the system. From her first day, Rima owned the space. She put on her shorts and tank top and joined the basketball games in the courts, just as she had done in her previous school, despite the stares she got from the boys adjusting to having a girl in their midst. "These are short shorts," Mona would tease, chuckling over the looks Rima was getting, "but you sure have the legs for them." Rima would roll her eyes. "It's just basketball," she would say, although she, too, enjoyed the attention. Never one to put on makeup or dress up the way other girls in Beirut did, she had often felt overshadowed by Mona and her girlfriends.

Fadi was in their orbit, but not yet anything more than another boy in a group of friends making their way through high school. Upon graduating, Fadi went to the American University of Beirut (AUB), Rima to another university, while Mona went to a public college, and that should have been the end of that. A year later, however, Rima decided to transfer to AUB with her friend Mary. They were sitting in line at the registration office, Mary grumbling about the tedious process, when a young man with an impressive hairdo and skinny white jeans—"too skinny," Rima recalls—bounded over to them. After reconnecting with Rima—"too excited," she says, "he was too excited"—Fadi offered to take over their paperwork. "I've done this before," he boasted. "I know how it works."

Rima and Mary looked at each other with a sly smile, handed over their files, and went to sit at Milk Bar, the campus café, to wait for him to get everything sorted. An hour in, Mary went to meet her boyfriend. Rima picked up a book to read. Eventually, Fadi returned, chest swollen with pride, and handed the completed forms back. "Really nice to see you again," he said. "It is," she replied. "You up for a drink at Talk of the Town?" he asked. She nodded and they made their way through the main gates on Bliss Street.

◆ ◆ ◆

Rima walks out of the English department into blinding sunlight. She says bye to her classmates and makes her way down the steps connecting the top of campus, near Main Gate, to sea level, past the engineering, pharmaceutical, and science schools. She's meeting Fadi outside the business school after his lecture. They have been dating for a few months. "Nothing serious," Rima tells Mona. "We're not exclusive or anything, but there's a lot of hanky panky!" The relationship is intense, oscillating between periods of closeness and space. Recurrent disagreements plague them. During her first year at AUB, Rima became a member of the student council, one of two women in a male-heavy space. "Do you have to work with all these guys?" Fadi keeps asking. His possessiveness was, to her, more manageable than his other objection: Palestine. "Isn't it time to let go of this?" he nagged. "As far as he's concerned," she recounts to her friend, "that's all part of our history; there's no way to turn back time. What's done is done. We are just different creatures," she explains. "We're having fun now, but it probably won't be anything more than that."

He walks out of his lecture, his flared jeans slung low on his waist. She, too, is wearing flared jeans and a tank top, big, brown sunglasses covering her face. She gives him a kiss on the cheek and, hand in hand, they walk into the tunnel that crosses under the Corniche and onto AUB's private beach. High fences rise behind them, blocking their view of the busy road above and preventing those on the Corniche from ogling the sunbathing bodies or jumping down onto the campus's beach. It is a tiny stretch of coast, severed from the mainland, an island floating in the middle of the sea, loosely tethered to Beirut.

The beach is not sandy. Big, black boulders descend into the water, each its own mountain that groups of students conquer. During most afternoons in the summer term, it is heaving with students. People are stretched out on the rocks, sunbathing. Others are playing cards, backgammon, smoking argileh, or shooting beach tennis—the sound of the ball bouncing off wooden rackets blends into the background. Music is blasting from someone's stereo as a few students dance in the sunlight, beer bottles reflecting the glare. Fadi pulls Rima to the quieter side of the beach, where a few people are reading. "This is your crew," he mocks her, pointing to a woman with a pile of books stacked next to her beach towel. She punches him lightly on the arm. "Yes, and that's yours." She points to a bunch of men on their knees, drunkenly clapping as a woman dressed in a skimpy bikini belly dances. He laughs, shrugs his shoulders, settles on a spot, and spreads his towel on a flat surface.

The rock is burning hot, but they're close to the waves, which splash cool water on them as they lie down, her head on his chest. "I'll get tan lines the shape of your face," he jokes. They doze off, the sun warming their bodies, the sound of traffic from the road above mixing with the noises of a beach day. Summer stretches ahead of them with no real plans. Fadi's job as a lifeguard is about to start, his responsibility to earn for his family acute. She has not yet decided what she wants to do, beyond spending more time with Mona, whom she has barely seen since she started at AUB. Fadi fidgets under her, sweaty. "Shall we dip in?"

They walk to the edge of the rock. He dives straight in. She climbs down. "Careful of the moss," he shouts, "you're going to slip. And the sea urchins! You'll step on one again! Just dive." She flaps her arm at him. *Ssssh*. The image of the first time he had taken her from al-Hadath to the beach where his father went diving for urchins floats into her mind. Her stepping on a sea urchin, him carrying her out of the water, lying her down, leaning in, studiously taking out each splinter. When he had finished, he pulled out a glove from his backpack, ran back to the water, dived in. He came back with another urchin in his palm. "What did you do that for?" she asked, giggling. "Revenge," he said, cutting it open with his pocketknife and offering it to her, smirking. She shook her head. He shrugged, spooning it in his mouth. "Yum." He smacked his lips, shaking his full head of hair all over her body before pulling her back in.

"Just dive," he's shouting now. She takes the plunge. "I hate the sea urchins," she laughs, swimming into his arms. "Yes, I know, but they're yummy," he says. She crinkles her nose, goes underwater, and with long, confident strokes, swims out into the sea. "I'm going to swim down the coast to Palestine one day," she once joked to him. "Lower your voice," he said, looking around.

9

BABA'S gamble paid off. His firm, wobbly at first, steadied itself and began to grow. "To succeed in life," he would tell my brothers and me, "you must do what you love." And his love was clear. It was a love of the sea that began in Beirut and manifested itself in his new office in this desert town with his father's scuba suit, replete with the glass bulb, hanging from the ceiling behind his desk. A relic from the past, disembodied. As his maritime business grew, we moved out of al-Abdali into a house on the western side of the city. West Amman, with its imposing houses and well-maintained facades, looked nothing like al-Abdali, gritty and overcrowded. Although a twenty-minute drive away, it was like relocating to another city. From our new neighborhood, Amman seemed vast, *rich*, with expansive streets, manicured front gardens, and endless backyards. The chaos of the east receded, its yellowed and stained limestone giving way to polished white exteriors. Before our eyes, Amman morphed into a grand city, nestled in its seven hills, imposing, unfazed.

"Look at this house," Baba proudly stated the day we moved in. "All our stuff is already in here and it still feels empty." He turned to us, eyes sparkling, and pulled a cigar from his jacket pocket, achieving his fantasy of graduating from cigarettes. He lit it and puffed away, christening the house. "الله يحميكم" Tata went around mumbling, blessing the house and reciting prayers. Mama, too, seemed satisfied; having hustled for years to support Baba's venture, she could relax. "Do you think we should get leather sofas for the sitting room?" she asked smugly, jokingly, aware that she did not quite fit the pretenses of West Amman. Laith, Nadim, and I each had our own room. I could finally line my walls with shelves to hold all the books I had stacked under my bed in al-Abdali. Laith rushed to hang up a basketball hoop in the back. We turned the basement into a playroom, nagging until it was furnished with a Ping-Pong table and video-games carousel.

The move happened the year I turned eleven, shortly before Easter, which is when we sometimes went down to the seaside in al-Aqaba. But when we stayed in Amman, as we did that year, we attended the Saturday of Light services, one of the happiest rituals for Tata. It was therefore, by default, one of the happiest rituals for me, and I enthusiastically got swept up in the three-day drama. It began with Good Friday, when very often the skies turned unusually gray and rainy. "Weepy," Tata said. That Friday was no exception. "The universe is in mourning," she explained. "Every Good Friday, the skies cry. What other miracle do we need to believe that Jesus is our God?" I grew tired, slumped my shoulders, imagined His death, mimicked Tata's mourning. Laith threw sidelong glances at me, rolled his eyes, poked my stomach to get me out of my funk as I moped around the house.

On Saturday, we slept in because the night ahead was long. By around 10 p.m., we dressed in our church outfits and went to the Church of the Virgin Mary. Like most Christian Ammanis, Baba, Nadim, and Laith only attended church on religious holidays or formal occasions—baptisms, weddings, funerals. Only Mama, Tata, and I went every Sunday. For me, those Sundays were not only occasions for dressing up—which I appreciated—but more importantly, they were sacred moments for communing with Jesus. But there was little communion to be had around Easter. The Saturday of Light was as much a social outing as a religious one; everyone in our small community congregated in the outside foyer of the church, chatting while the rituals proceeded in the background.

The Mass started outdoors in the night chill as the church turned, in our collective imagination, into Christ's tomb in the hills around Jerusalem. We were the believers standing at the entrance to the cave, in mourning, knocking on the stony walls, seeking his body. The priest, flanked by young boys, rapped on the church door while reciting prayers and burning incense, his voice mournful as it carried over the heads of the faithful. Baba picked me up so I could see. More knocking as I imagined a huge wooden rod being rammed against the door, echoing out into the cavernous space inside. The prayers went on and on, an impassioned ritual of grief that knotted itself in my stomach.

Mama stood next to Baba, crossing her face every now and then, praying. Tata looked ahead, impassive. Laith and Nadim were behind the crowds, playing with other kids.

I followed the priest's movements, and as the clocks struck midnight, the doors were flung open. I gasped. A sea of candles inside the church threw its orange light onto our stricken faces. Instead of a corpse, there was fire, and a sense of salvation that was contagious. قام المسيح, the crowd murmured. The light began to spread among us as each person lit the candle in their hand. Baba lit one for us both. Swiftly, my morbidity gave way to joy. *Christ has risen!* The crowd shuffled into the church, a hallowed space, one that had defied death, and had come ablaze with life, burning away the sins we are born with, those lodged into our very being.

The following morning, Easter Sunday, we woke up late and got ready for lunch at our cousin's house. I locked myself in the bathroom and embarked on a multi-hour operation of grooming and outfit try-ons. There was a single mirror hanging over the sink, forcing me to climb onto the pink bidet to get a full-body view. It was all taking a bit longer than I had anticipated. Barely one outfit in and Mama had knocked on the door to ask if I was OK—everyone was already dressed. I quickly tried on a few more, crunched my curls up, and settled on a brightly colored, flowy silk shirt with a black elastic waistband that fit snugly over my white shorts, the origins of which I cannot recall. I looked like a young guest star on the set of *The Golden Girls*, the show Tata and I often tuned in to after lunch.

Mama and Baba stared at me as I eventually exited the bathroom and, speechless, let me trail behind them out of the house and into the car, where my brothers and Tata were waiting. We made our way to our cousin's house and let ourselves straight into the kitchen, where the women had gathered.

"Christ has risen," my cousin's mother declared as she greeted us.

"Indeed he has!" we all responded in unison.

She leaned in to kiss my parents, engulfing me in a cloud of rose-infused perfume, distinctly like my own. After one or two perplexed comments on the shirt, my desire to make an entrance fizzled. Instead, I eyed the spread on the counter, but held back from the feast. The mahshi was piled high. A large platter with lamb chunks resting in rice and with roasted pine nuts and almonds on top sat at the center. The omnipresent bowl of fettuccine was placed next to a fattoush salad. I resisted smuggling away a fried kubbeh as Nadim and I ran up the stairs to find my cousin Issam. Laith followed Baba into the living room, where the men congregated, drinking arak and smoking cigars.

Upstairs, Issam, who was a couple of years younger than me, was absorbed in a *Sonic the Hedgehog* game and thoroughly uninterested in the guests arriving. He waved us over, with a swift glance to acknowledge our presence. Nadim dove straight in. I settled into one of the armchairs, arranging my silk shirt just so, and tried to make sense of what was happening on the screen before promptly losing interest. I wanted us to go and play with the neighborhood kids in the cul-de-sac outside. After a couple of rounds on the Sega, I wore them down.

We played hide-and-seek, and the afternoon passed in a blaze of counting, crawling through the bushes, and squeezing under the metal trash containers lining the end of the street, where pebbles on the asphalt tore through my smeared white shorts. We ran in and out of the house, the guests milling about, providing fertile grounds for hiding, crouched behind curtains and under tables. At some point, we huddled on the front lawn to discuss new rules. We decided that winners needed to impose truth-or-dare punishments on losers. Since secrets hardly made sense to us, we chose challenges that became, with every round, more daring. Winners told losers to run around the house three times; to go up to parents in the middle of the dining hall and swear loudly; to smell sweaty socks. My silk shirt, oversized and drenched with sweat, was getting in the way. I took it off and borrowed a T-shirt from Issam before playing some more.

We broke for lunch. I piled my plate high and sat in the corner, picking at my food. My heart was beating fast and my glasses were foggy, but heat was not the reason I had suddenly lost my appetite. A thought had floated into my mind, out of nowhere, and I did not quite know what to make of it. In the frenzy of planning where my next hideout was going to be, and with the pride of realizing that no one had yet thought of sneaking into the bedrooms upstairs, I realized that—actually—I wanted to lose. *I want Issam to win. I want him to offer me a challenge. I want to be told what to do.* My body tingled. A sense of foreboding—strange, unfamiliar—added to the tingles. *There are people around us. We could be seen.* Doing what, exactly, I was not sure. My mind burst with images, of *Sayida Mil'aqa*, of "pillows" with Khalo, of the possibilities that now presented themselves—shrunken or not—of playing with other boys. I was presumptuous, arrogant, knowing with untested certainty that I could get Issam to do my bidding, even when my bidding was to do his. Nervous, also; "pillows" had to remain unwitnessed in darkened rooms, where I thrived. Here, in Amman's daytime, this intrusion of fantasy into reality would happen in full sight of everyone. I trembled.

Lunch and dessert flew by, the games resumed, and, barely a few minutes in, I was facing off with Issam.

"Is that the worst you can do?" I heard myself taunting him. "Sure, I can smell your socks. That's easy."

The other kids were in hiding. Issam and I were panting, our stomachs full of food, feeling a bit nauseous in the heat. My chest swelled with pride at my ability to orchestrate things with very little effort. I was a master manipulator, filled with anticipation, with firm knowledge that I was standing on the cusp of something new.

"I can do worse. Much worse!" he protested.

"No you can't. We smelled socks! You can't think of anything else. You're just a silly boy."

"I can make you smell my underwear!"

"With you in them?"

My thick glasses are flung sideways on the lawn next to me. My T-shirt is sweaty, and I am out of breath, lying on my back. Issam is straddling my face in his crunchy green briefs. The spring's untrimmed grass is tickling the back of my neck and my ears, a sensation printed indelibly on my mind.

10

بين ليلة وضحاها—as Mama says. Between a night and its dawn, the schoolyard that had once enticed me became a confusing place, a menacing one. There was nothing unusual about that morning. Baba had left for work and Mama was getting ready for hers, both leaving Tata to tidy up and prepare lunch. Mama hassled us into the car. "Seatbelts on," she instructed as she drove through Amman's morning rush and into Shmeisani. "What a smart idea, putting a school in the middle of the business district"—every morning the same complaint, forgetting in her grumbling that she and Baba were the ones who had chosen the school despite its busy location. "The best private school in the city," they claimed. This was not quite right, but it was certainly the best they could afford, and it was the one that all their friends sent their kids to. She dropped us off by the back entrance, and we rushed out, weaving our way through rows of honking cars.

We split up as soon as we entered the gates and ran into assembly, where I made my way to the fifth-grade lineup and Nadim to the first grade. We sang the national anthem as Laith joined the older tenth-grade boys hoisting up the flag at the front. I stood straight, feeling very solemn, shoulders pulled back, the fingers of my right hand stiff against my temple, mouthing the lyrics, making my declaration to our king.

عاش المليك, عاش المليك
سامياً مقامهُ
خافقاتٍ في المعالي أعلامهُ

Maya, standing in front of me, turned to wave, smiling widely, showing off the gap in her front teeth. And I could see the back of Issa's head at the front of the lineup, taller than any of us—almost double our size—and hairier by far. After the anthem, we walked up the stairs together to class, where Maya and I sat next to each other on our classroom's two-person benches, and Issa had a whole one to himself behind us. It was a day like any other. Yet, after the recess bell rang and the kids flooded down the stairs into the courtyard, everything was altered somehow. Mocking stares. Eyes filled with disgust. Lips pursed a bit too tightly. Mouth corners curled ever so slightly. Kind eyes averted.

These looks that I encountered may have been there all along, unnoticed, until that day: the first day I felt what I would come to call the darting shadows. Looks that were fleeting, furtive, impossible to dismiss, equally impossible to pin down. Glances that communicated more truthfully than any of the clumsy words that often followed.

Darting shadows began accompanying me everywhere in Amman. Jumping at me from every encounter: in the market; from the passenger in the car next to us in traffic; the school bus driver; the kids playing football in the alley; the salesman I bought trousers from; Mama's friends; Baba's business associates. Throughout any day, masochistically, I committed to confronting the darting shadows. Never to provoke, just to take note of them. Like a harvester walking through the fields, plucking their crops and shoving them into a bag slung over their shoulder. A bag that bulged and grew heavier with each harvest. I looked around, reaping the shadows, hating them, etching them into my mind, carving them into my skin.

◆ ◆ ◆

I am standing by the blue railings that frame the flights of stairs leading to the courtyard. I linger, debating whether to pull myself onto the ledge and read my book or brave it down to recess. I pause, unsure. I start examining the railing. I peel off patches of paint to expose the metal beneath, then stop and rest my palm against it, skin to metal that has been sizzling in Amman's sun. The scalding pain shoots up my arm. I tighten my grip until the pain turns into a dull throb. I take out the sandwich that Tata has prepared for me and placed in a Ziploc bag, labneh with sliced cucumber and olive oil, and nibble. The bread is soggy from the heat, the paper napkin it is wrapped in tinged a hue of green. I spot Maya, put the sandwich away, hurry down the steps, and stand next to her on the edge of the playground.

I want to tell my younger self to stay where he is, to lean against the ledge, to read instead. But a chasm separates us, one I have worked hard to put in place. Still, I cannot avoid reliving this moment alongside him, as I see Mustapha Aboud from the corner of my eye. That was his name. An unwelcome memory greedily taking up space in my mind. The power those kids have over me respects no boundaries, not even time. *Do those tormentors remember my name, or am I the only one charged with remembering theirs?* I imagine there is stillness in their mind, chaos in mine, as I am burdened with all the details about them I do not care to recall. His scrawny body. His thick, curly hair. His pointed nose.

Mustapha Aboud. My eyes avoided his because eye contact was an invitation. There were times when he did not require even that to head my way. I see an overweight kid with curly black hair standing in the middle of a circle of jeering and laughing boys. Although my height, Mustapha towers over me.

"I'll fuck you and your sister if you push into me again. Next time you see me pass, you stop and get out of the way يا خول. Do you understand me, you fucking faggot?"

I do not trust my voice. Do not know how to tell him I have no sister.

"You don't know how to answer me? Let me show you. You hold your hand up like this," he says, as he puts one hand on his hip, which he juts out dramatically to the side, and holds the other up so that his wrist flops over, "and you say, 'Yes, of course, whatever you say, sir. I will get out of the way. I'm sorry.'"

He says this in a high-pitched voice that makes my ears heat up and my temples throb so loudly I almost do not hear the shrieking laughter from the boys around me. *Do they not know that I, too, find these gestures monstrous? That I, too, want to shed them? Do they not understand that I, too, want to be on the other side of the circle instead of standing here in the middle?* With nowhere to go, I imagine shrinking my body, making myself so small as to be invisible, indetectable. And as I see his limp wrist, I instantly snap my own. My tendons stretch to attention. A quiet act of rebellion, to show him, to show everyone around him, that he is lying. My wrist is not limp. I try to straighten my back, too, but a weight pulls my shoulders down, slumps me forward as my cheeks burn. I look at the boys around me in that circle. Some appear delighted, their eyes fixed onto mine, asserting their dominance without having to touch me. Others refuse to make contact, looking away as they remain rooted in place, the spectacle too enthralling for them to leave.

I feel my mouth dry as I stand surrounded, looking into his black eyes, imploring him to move on, or at least to find another corner to stage his performance. A corner where my brothers are not able to see. I do not want them to know who I am, to witness what Mustapha will soon reveal. I do not want them to tell Mama and Baba. I look up and my eyes lock onto a pair of gray eyes. His eyes. Ramzi's. I single him out, even back then, because I know who he is. Even though we have never met, or so I thought at the time, I know we have a family connection, and I worry that, through him, word of this will reach Baba and Mama. I look in his direction, pleading for discretion, seeking clues as to what he might tell his parents, if anything. He smirks and I understand. He is in on the game. The taunting continues.

"Do you get me, little girl?"

My tongue is lost. I nod, looking at the black asphalt of the courtyard until Mustapha Aboud moves on, shoving me aside as he walks off, followed by the others. The physical collision is barely perceptible and hardly memorable compared to the jolt inside me. The searing shame I felt at having been humiliated.

Maya and Issa reemerge from their hideouts and come over, pretending that nothing has happened. I am grateful. There is the last shred of dignity in that pretense. I am grateful, also, that they still choose to sit with me, even after my ugliness has been so expertly laid bare. That offers some relief as I return to the blue railing to guide me up the steps, supporting me as my knees threaten to give way. One step up and my mind starts whirring, weaving over this memory with an alternate reality, a different day in school that I will tell Mama and Baba about over lunch. One in which I read my book on the ledge, or was showered in compliments from my teachers. I embody this reality, retreat into it, and in that way begin to disappear.

At night, I enter my bedroom, shut the door, and kneel by my bed, knees on the hard, cold tiles. I start with the Lord's Prayer, which I know Laith and Nadim are also reciting in their rooms, as we all did when we shared a single room in al-Abdali. I also know that before I am even halfway through, they will have scrambled into their beds. I stay put and press my forehead into the lush velvet of my duvet. A deep blue that turns light when stroked against the grain. My breath is humid, damp, accumulating in front of my face, my cheeks hot against the soft cover. My palms are clutched and settled in my lap.

I begin. I remove the burdensome bag of darting shadows I have been hauling around and, one by one, replay the episodes of my day, reflecting on what I did to provoke each strike. Tata insisted that we do not need mediators to speak to God. "Priests are men, like us," she said. "They are just as full of sin. We can offer our souls directly to the Almighty, without having to go to church or to the confessional stand," she instructed, "and He will receive us just the same if we come with pure intentions." And that is what I am doing. Coming with pure intentions. I am confessing, seeking not only solace through my prayers, but, also, urgently, desperately, forgiveness. I know that my failures, my being, reek of sin, and that forgiveness is necessary. It is an ugliness residing within me that provokes the darting shadows. That knowledge rests in the pit of my stomach, immovable, solid, ever-present.

My mind quiets, like a refrigerator that stops its hum, as it focuses on the task at hand. I must run through the list fixed in my mind to earn my right to get into bed. *Forgive me, Jesus, for I have sinned. I am now making a promise to God that this is the last time I ask for a doll, laugh like a girl, play pillows with Khalo, or hide-and-seek that way....* A ritual to cleanse myself before sleeping. With each episode I pull up, replay, my body flushes with shame. I *want* my body to flush with shame. It is shame that I deserve, that I must feel again, to prove that I am sincere in my pursuit of absolution.

Madness ensues. An internal chanting fills my mind. Words that play incessantly, relentlessly, for years. Lines that are recited aloud when I am alone and whispered when I am around other people. *Forgive me, Jesus, for I have sinned. I am now making a promise to God that this is the last time....* The mantra plays itself out until exhaustion takes over. I get up, my knees stiff and my legs cold, and slide under the duvet.

11

RIMA had been drifting from Lubna and Abdullah since starting at university, even as she and Mona stayed close, partying, flirting with boys, riding on the backs of mopeds around the city, down to the beach or up to the mountains for lunches that turned into dinners. A hedonistic bliss that, for a while, at least, kept at bay the signs in the city around them, the whispers that proliferated with every encounter, the percolating awareness that Beirut was veering toward the abyss. Tata continued to refuse to believe that the country they had landed in after Palestine was on the brink of violence. But Rima could feel it in the air around her, and more immediately, in her own neighborhood, especially in Tal al-Zaatar. As one of the only camps in the Christian area of East Beirut, Tal al-Zaatar was reviled. For the right-wing Christian Phalange, its mere existence proved that the predominantly Muslim Palestinian refugees who had landed in Lebanon after the Nakba were the reason their country was disintegrating. Violent clashes took place with increasing frequency in and around the camp, and weeks would often go by when Rima could barely get any news of Mona, let alone see her. Those weeks, the tension solidified like a rock in her body.

It was well known that Palestinian fighters were training in Tal al-Zaatar, amassing weapons for their struggle, their war to liberate Palestine and return home. And she suspected this was partly why Lubna and Abdullah had become more withdrawn, more secretive. As skirmishes around the camp escalated, she and Mona decided to sign up for medical training. They talked to Abdullah, who arranged everything. Nothing advanced, just some tips on first aid interventions and basic self-defense they might need. She didn't tell Fadi. He already thought she spent too much of her time organizing for Palestine. Having risen to the position of secretary at the student council by the time she was in her final year at AUB in 1975, she was at the forefront of protests on campus. And now that her final year coincided with unrest in the city, Fadi was particularly nervous about the implications of Rima's activism. He would not have approved of this training. In any case, to her and Mona, the work they were doing with the Palestinian fighters was almost a game, a fantasy, a preparation for a battle that they could not quite imagine participating in.

Until one morning in the summer of 1976, when the Phalangist militiamen—dressed in brown, orange-tinged army fatigues and light brown T-shirts, rifles slung over their shoulders—put Tal al-Zaatar under siege. They had done this before: surrounded the camp, intimidated it, blocked off supplies to it. But this was different. All along the camp's entrances, metal barriers were erected, a border where none existed before. Flimsy structures that could have easily been swept aside if it weren't for the soldiers standing behind them, their idle but confident postures confirmation of what everyone knew: The country was in a civil war, and the Palestinian refugees were in the middle of it. The possibility of battle no longer seemed so distant.

This siege was total. Nobody could enter or leave. No food. No medicine. No water in the middle of Beirut's summer. The militias began actively invading the camp, battling with the fighters and terrorizing its residents. Overnight, the tension in the city—the heated exchanges and bloody scuffles, the charged air—had manifested these militias down the street from her home.

Rima could not get into the camp anymore and Mona was unable to leave. It was too dangerous for her, not just to slip out, but also to be seen entering Rima's house. A casual crossing of the street, a friendship, had become incriminating. Rima was Palestinian, but not like them, those masses languishing behind the metal barriers, out of view, and now out of contact. She wondered when, and how, she would see Mona. She fretted about her friends and their families, about the provisions they needed, and constantly sought news as to whether they had survived the bloody attacks the militias were leading. On the first night of the siege, when she walked into her bedroom, there was a note on her bedside table: *Don't come to us. I'll let you know when it's safe to meet. M.*

Throughout university, Rima lived at home in Hazmieh. Every morning, she got into her little car, a beat-up, blue, sixties Renault, and drove down to AUB. On the way, depending on which route she took, she passed several refugee camps—Burj al-Barajneh, Sabra, Shatila, Mar Elias—flimsy camps that were undeniably getting concretized as the decades following 1948 rolled by. After her training, without telling Tata or Fadi, she began missing some of her classes and volunteering at Mar Elias, Sabra, and Shatila. She could not recall when she had made the decision to start. One day, she found herself parking across the street and walking in. *How could I be sitting in class as if nothing of consequence was happening in the city?* Even though she was an English major and only had basic medical training, she was drafted where she was most needed: first aid support and health-care services at the Red Crescent clinic, where the nurses were dangerously understaffed.

She tried to assuage her guilt in those camps. She knew her efforts were inconsequential in the grander scheme of things. She imagined she was helping Mona, her family, and this calmed her. Made her feel like she was in control again. The listlessness that ate away at her on campus subsided in the camps, giving her some relief, space to breathe. *Funny*, she thought to herself often, *it was the campus, the American campus, that was meant to offer this relief.* The university was supposed to act as a haven, insulated from the violence that had erupted around it over the last year. Most actors involved in the war—armed militias and government forces—treated it as a neutral place, so that the campus provided reprieve from the looting, kidnapping, shelling, and snipers that were everywhere in the city. They never entered the university's zone. At least, they were not meant to. But for her, these camps—where she glimpsed the fedayeen fighters rushing down the alleyways, women cooking and watching over the kids in their single-room homes, where she walked down tight alleys with the posters of martyrs plastered on the walls—it was here that the chaos around her made sense.

She took this energy onto campus with her, to the protests she and other students were organizing. *For Palestinian rights! For liberation! For ending Israel's occupation! For stopping Zionist crimes! For the right of return!* Disrupting the normalcy of student life to remind everyone that everything was not normal: a generation on, and refugees were nowhere closer to getting their homes back. Now that this issue was at the forefront of the numerous other issues in their fracturing city, her organizing work was more important than ever—and, for Fadi, more threatening. This was the time to focus on her final year, to graduate and move on, he thought. Nothing could be further from her mind.

One morning that summer, after working at the clinic, she walked out of the camp and got into her car to head to university. She pulled out into traffic, the pickup truck behind her honking loudly. She flung her arm out of the window, flicking him off, before sensing that her car's balance was off. She found a spot by the curb a few meters ahead and pulled back in. She got out to inspect the tires. Everything was fine on her side. She walked over to the passenger side and saw that one of the tires was deflated. Not deflated—punctured. The Swiss Army knife was still firmly lodged in it. She stood on the side of the road, staring at it for a long time, knowing that if she looked up, she would see the knife's owner looking back at her. Those messages had been coming in with greater urgency, with more forceful determination and open hostility toward Palestinians, especially those active in the camps. Aware that she was being watched, she picked up her bag from the front seat, locked the car, left the knife in the tire, and hailed a service cab to Hamra. There was a protest to go to on campus.

◆ ◆ ◆

It was a particularly scorching week when Abu Issa forced his way into Rima's house, demanding money. Beirut was in the middle of its August heat wave, and Rima's summer term—her final one—was about to end. Tal al-Zaatar had been under siege for close to two months, since June, and the fighting was getting fiercer with every passing week. Greater numbers of civilian refugees were escaping, carrying with them horrific news of the atrocities the militias were committing. Rima kept hoping Mona and her family, too, would find a way out. As was often the case, before days of heavy fire between the Phalange and Palestinian guerillas, Mona would send Rima a note. *Stay inside tonight.* Or

Take shelter in the basement. Or *Leave if you can.* Their little flat on the incline was in the crossfire between the two warring parties, and most of the building's floors had evacuated as Lebanese families fled to the mountains. Mona's warnings were heeded carefully. "الله يحميهم" Tata started saying, aware that Mona's messages were keeping them safe. At a time when the men in her family were abroad, she held onto Mona as their guardian angel. The angel that He, in His mysterious ways, had sent them.

And for Rima, the messages were proof of life. With no food, water, or medicine, how could people live? Every meal she had now was a reminder of meals her friends couldn't have. Rage swelled in her body. One day, Rima got into her car, as usual, and headed out to campus, wondering when she might see Mona next, to hug and thank her. Wondering whether it was Mona or one of their other comrades who was leaving the notes for her in different places. Lost in thought, she almost did not notice the man waving by the side of the road as she was about to turn in to al-Hamra. He looked familiar, but she couldn't put her finger on where she had seen him. She slowed down and pulled over. He leaned into the passenger window. "Comrade, turn around, they're arresting the Palestinian students." He walked off before she could ask any questions. *How did he know who she was? Who was arresting the students, and how many had been arrested? How had they dared to enter the university grounds? And what will happen to her courses?* This was her final semester. She was due to graduate that fall. Her mind filled with unanswered questions, but she knew not to question the orders. She made a U-turn in the middle of the busy street and drove back to Hazmieh.

The Phalangists were becoming more brazen in their attacks, more active in suppressing Palestinians, whether activists or fighters or both. After that knife in her tire, and being recognized on the street, Rima was uncomfortable. Fadi had told her to take a back seat, to quiet down, and at the time, she had meant it when she had promised him she would. But how could she back down when Mona was the one locked in a camp? Over the next few days, she got updates on what was happening on campus from classmates, from Fadi, from other friends.

She heard that one hundred students had been arrested, taken into custody or expelled from university, but she had no way to confirm. *I would have been the 1 in 101, expelled because I had protested for a just cause*, she kept thinking as she busied herself around the house. Helping with chores, unusually acquiescent. It was hard to breathe. "It's like there's a brick on my chest," she kept telling Tata. It was not because of Beirut's humid heat, which made them feel like they were swimming in a warm shower as they went about their day. The tension in the air was unbearable, and it was as if everything in her body was telling her to resist her urges, to stay put, to fight her impulses in order to avoid getting anyone into trouble.

By early August, discussions were under way to end the siege on the camp. The water supplies had dwindled to dangerously low levels and the fighters inside were negotiating their surrender. They would lay down their rifles, and the civilians left behind would be allowed safe passage. That was reportedly the agreement, and she could not wait. She would waltz right up to Mona's house, give her mother a hug, see Lubna and Abdullah, kiss their hands for all that they had done for her and Tata. Everyone was coming back to their senses.

On the eve of the lifting of the siege, the night of August 11, fearsome noises burst out of the camp, threatening whatever dreams she might have harbored of a peaceful outcome. The loud explosions had woken her in the middle of the night. Tata's diaries record that night, too: *Black night. Missiles hitting. It's terribly bad.* Rima got out of bed and paced her bedroom, wanting to run out, knowing she should not. Tata had woken up, too. They huddled around the radio. *Clashes in Tal al-Zaatar* was all they could get as Tata whispered her prayers. The fedayeen were reportedly leaving. *Maybe these are the final clashes*, Rima thought. *Maybe they are getting ambushed by the militias on their way out.*

Come morning, on August 12, Rima prepared for the lifting of the siege, to go into the camp. She had shopped and got provisions. She would bring Mona and her family to stay at their house for a while, to recover. She would hold her. She waited all day for news from her friend, but there was only silence. Some refugees were trickling out of the camp's various entrances, but there was no word from Mona or her family. Then the updates started surfacing. Throughout that day, after the fighters had left and the remaining civilians were defenseless, despite the agreement to allow them safe passage out, something had gone horribly wrong. It happened swiftly. The Phalangists could not resist the temptation. They had seized their chance and gone into the camp instead. A massacre. Hundreds of Palestinians. Bodies everywhere. The stench of death. Murdered after being starved for fifty-three days. Her neighborhood had become ground zero of the civil war.

The news, when it landed, altered Rima. She was neither inconsolable nor desperate. She was simply changed. In one fell swoop, her old self was no longer. Even before she was told, Rima knew. She knew that Mona and her family had been slaughtered. She knew she would be next. She knew her life in Beirut was over. As did Tata; reliving Deir Yassin, knowing that—like her father before her—it was now incumbent on her to get her daughter out. More bloodied hands, more lessons learned.

How quickly a life can be packed up. Rima sent a note to Fadi: *Come to Amman.* They gathered all they could into Rima's car and got in. Tata crouched in the leg space of the passenger seat as Rima drove them out of Hazmieh, careening toward the mountains, dodging sniper bullets, before blending into a UN convoy that was making its way out of Lebanon into Syria and eventually Jordan. The events of the past few days that had spurred them into action were only slowly making their way through their bodies, not to be recollected or recounted for many years to come. Stories remain untold about the days between Abu Issa's intrusion and Mama and Tata's flight to Amman. A darkness that crosses Mama's face tells me some memories are best left untouched.

Fadi followed soon after. Even in the aftermath of Tal al-Zaatar, he was convinced the country would pull itself from the brink. He assured his parents and sister that he would be back. He needed to travel to Amman to check on Rima and, equally importantly, find employment.

Now that he had graduated, he could earn more and provide for them, until the situation in Lebanon stabilized and he could find himself a good job there.

In Amman, they all crammed into the house of Tata's brother-in-law, Rima's uncle, who had fled from Jerusalem to Jordan in 1948 and had become a well-connected politician. He was to intervene, to work his networks and get them temporary residencies to stay. "Amman is not Beirut," he cautioned from the very beginning. "Things have to change." Theirs was a conditional residency. "You are allowed to remain in Amman," he stressed, "as long as there is no more funny business on Palestine. The government will not risk another Black September." It was a message directed at Rima. One she received silently, broken. *How could there ever be funny business again?* Mona was dead. Abdullah and Lubna, she found out, had survived the massacre and fled to Gaza. She was unsure when—if—she would ever see them again. *What funny business could there possibly be without any of her people?*

This was not the only thing that had to change. In Amman, everything was *3eib*, that unforgiving indictment that dictates what people can or cannot do, how they can or cannot be. The city ran on the mutterings of disapproval, uttered when someone did something improper. What that thing was, the action that evoked dishonor, was inconsequential. What mattered was whether it was seen, picked up by Amman's gossiping masses, the guardians of our morality, primed and ready to excise anyone who did not fit into the expected mold. In this instance, Rima and Fadi and their relationship, which in Beirut had been free, expansive, unbound by time and expectation, could no longer remain so. "If you're both living under my roof," Rima's uncle said, "this has to be formalized. This is not Beirut; people talk here. It is time for you both to get engaged."

Fadi had long wanted a marriage and now made his position clear. It was not really a conversation, more an acknowledgment of a fait accompli. "We are in Jordan," he said, "and we want to start a family. You don't want the kids to be harassed, do you? You don't want them to struggle to get nationality here, for that to become an impossible feat. Where would they go?"

How could she respond to these questions? Had she known that the U-turn away from her campus, which she had made barely a week before, would be her last chance to be at the university, maybe she would not have turned back. She might have kept going, driven to the protest, screamed and yelled, and yes, maybe even got imprisoned and beaten up. But she hadn't. She had retreated, and they had won. She would not get to graduate or finish her studies. She would not get to see her friends again.

A family? In this lifeless town? Maybe. The life she had imagined was never going to happen. Her comrades had been murdered. Maybe the only thing left to do was to lie low. To build an alternate reality with Fadi, where they could at least play at normalcy. Tata agreed. "What's done is done, *ya binti*. You want your children to go through this, for what? Learn from me, after Palestine, we too started new lives in Beirut." After catastrophe comes life and family. But did Rima desire those things? She no longer had the answers. She loved Fadi. Of course she did. And in this new city, after this news, the conviction that had driven her to protest came undone. Hers was a choice that was not really a choice. She followed in the steps laid out before her. Silence, resignation, residency, and marriage to a man she loved. A domesticated life. A good one, just not the life that she had imagined for herself. And the fire within her? Until she learned to control it, it burned in every direction around her.

12

THE smell of frying nudges me out of sleep. The sun is not yet up. I get out of bed and walk into the kitchen. Mama is at the stove, stirring sliced onions in olive oil on a low heat.

"Good morning, sleepyhead, you're up early."

Her tone is gentle, not yet hardened by the day. I give her a kiss, ask her what she's cooking.

"فاصولياء. Tata will prepare the rest," she says, "I'm just getting it started."

"When did you get up?"

"I've been up since four thirty. I couldn't sleep."

"You wake up so early," I yawn.

I go back and shake my brothers out of their sleep. We get ready for school and my body tenses. I put out my hands in front of me, raise four fingers on each. *The number of hours I will be gone*, I think to myself. *I can take down one finger each hour.* And I do, hour on hour, throughout the day, so that by the time I get back home, eight hours later, I put two fists in front of me. *Two big zeros.* I walk straight into the aroma of the green bean stew that Tata has cooked. Both she and Mama are in the kitchen. Mama is frustrated, I can tell, no longer the calm presence I had encountered at dawn, when the house was still and asleep. She is dressed in her work clothes and has an apron covering her skirt. I ask if she's OK. "Yes." She is curt with me, and I know better than to prod. I give Tata a hug.

"How was school?" she asks. I shrug and let my head rest on her shoulder.

"يا ابني، اتكل, 'Lay your worldly burdens at my feet,' Jesus Christ had instructed his beloved apostles," she says, rubbing my back.

I nod and leave the kitchen with the salad bowl. Baba is seated at the head of the table where we gathered every day at a time that was neither lunch nor quite dinner. I put the bowl down and give him a kiss. Mama follows with the rest of the food and takes her place to his right, close to the kitchen. Tata, seated beside me, reminds us to say grace. We clutch our hands in front of our faces and bow as Laith, the eldest, mumbles a prayer, the same one we turn to at every meal, reciting words that comfort only in their repetition, having lost all meaning over the years.

"Rima, can you get the salt?" Baba, dressed in his pajamas, ready for his siesta, mutters as soon as Laith finishes.

Mama, having just sat down, gets up. Laith begins talking about his basketball game at school, which I caught glimpses of from the landing above. Nadim watched the game and wants details. Baba listens, waiting for the salt, which he grabs from Mama, whose eyes meet mine. Laith is recounting how, close to the end of the first half, he was blocked from a perfect shot by his best friend, who was, unusually, he tells us, playing on the other side.

"He knew I was going to try that shot. He knows my moves too well."

"The food is too hot," Baba grumbles, pushing the plate away from himself in exasperation, making his fork and knife clatter. "Why can't you just take it off the stove twenty minutes before we get here?" he snaps, looking at Mama. "Is that so hard? *Ufft*."

Ufft. The mother of all expressions. A word so versatile it can be as innocuous as a casual exclamation of surprise, or—as was frequently the case with Baba—a threatening declaration of fury. A biting *ufft* from him could silence us for the remainder of the meal, or sometimes even condemn us to an evening of hushed conversations. The air crackles. Mama looks confused and says something about having turned off the stove a while back—as soon as she walked in from work.

"I'm sorry," she says, "I'll serve it cooler next time."

Baba, placated, pulls the plate closer to him again. The conversation tentatively restarts. It meanders, from the basketball game to Nadim's classes to mine. I mention a comment from our elementary English teacher about my comprehension skills, and Mama nods proudly across the table. We move on to Baba's day, which went well, to Mama's, which would often include some funny story about Ziad, her manager, a sweet but incompetent businessman who depended on her to do almost everything in the office without ever giving her credit. This time, she recounts how she had to sit down with a potential client while Ziad was out picking up his dry cleaning, having forgotten about the meeting, and of her almost closing the deal. Just as she was about to get a commitment from the client, she beams, Ziad burst into the office, flustered, with hangers and shirts flying about, and—

"Rima, you changed this recipe. I liked it more before," Baba interrupts her, holding his plate out for more.

Mama shoots an exasperated look across the table. She offers him a stiff serving of food and says something in defense, a futile effort, like "It's the same recipe" or "Have you noticed anything different, boys?" inviting one of us to protest Baba's verdict, to rally to her side. A practiced exchange; we have been here before. Our home is مكهرب, electrified, with a current that runs through our daily lives, as present and constant as the couch in our living room or the food we ate. I put my palms under my thighs and look down at my food. Next to me, Tata stiffens and works to dispel the tension, gently offering an antidote.

"I added more pepper," she says. "It needed spice."

I follow her lead, trying to inject levity.

"Hmm, really? I love this recipe. It's yummy. What did Ziad do, Mama?"

The conversation falters. Mama shakes her head as we eat the remainder of our meal quietly, our cutlery clanking against the plates.

"دايعة," Baba chirps after a few bites.

He gets up, leaving his plate on the table. The tension defuses, like a balloon losing air. I help Mama clear the dishes. Her frustration, palpable before lunch, does not erupt. She never fights back or lashes out at Baba, at least not in our presence. Instead, her anger is stoked, an ember that only occasionally—unpredictably—bursts into flame: at Amman's dust as she manically cleans the house; at shop attendants and strangers in the street; at everyone and everything around her that is doing something to ruin her day. A rage that has become a part of her being, one so essential that, without it, she would be lost, a traveler without a compass moving through an unforgiving life.

13

AS Lebanon's civil war subsided in the early nineties, fifteen years after their flight to Amman, and after much back-and-forth, Baba and Mama decided to take us to Beirut to spend the summer with Tata Marcel, Baba's mother. Having refused to flee, Tata Marcel had featured in our lives primarily as a staticky voice—the older woman my brothers and I were forced to speak to in the infrequent times Baba could get through. "تقبرني حبيبي," she would say on the phone, over and over again, leaving me wondering why this strange woman was asking me to bury her. I was curious about her, as she had stuck out the war by herself, but I was more intrigued by the neighborhood where she lived, al-Hamra. "The street is full of cafés and secondhand bookstores," Mama told me every time she drove us to the one bookstore in Amman's first circle, on yet another mission to purchase more books for me to read. "You can get lost in endless libraries and spend the day reading by the side of the road, watching people go by." The way my parents spoke of Beirut made it seem colorful, compared to Amman's gray. I wanted to visit this famed street, to buy books, to sit in bustling cafés, to explore the city where my parents had met and fallen in love.

In the days leading to the trip, my parents got more and more animated. Mama pulled out piles of photo albums that had gathered dust. "Wait till you see how beautiful it is," she said, describing AUB. In one of the pictures, the two of them are standing in front of College Hall, an imposing four-story building topped by the university's iconic watchtower. Mama is dressed in tight, high-waisted jeans, a tank top, and large sunglasses, her hair curly and voluminous. Baba's jeans are also tight on the hips and flared into elephant feet, his shirt fitted and tucked in, the upper buttons open to reveal a hairy chest. My brothers and I laughed when we first saw the picture, more elated by how happy the two of them looked than by their past fashion choices. The tower,

Mama explained, suppressing giggles herself, overlooked the sea and AUB's beach. "We skipped class and spent whole afternoons swimming and sunbathing on the seafront strip that the campus owned," she said. "It wasn't a sandy beach or anything. It was rocky; big boulders in the water. But back then, we just lazed on the rocks, it didn't matter."

A few weeks before our scheduled departure day, a bomb went off on AUB's campus, killing two people. "It's devastating," Mama said, as she worried the war might reignite. She had learned not to heed promises of peace. And this trip to Beirut was bringing up long-suppressed memories. She had fled a grieving activist; she was returning a resigned mother. She and Baba went into a tailspin. *Should we go, should we not?* The promise of a ceasefire had been dangled in front of them one time too many, and anyway there was never any certainty about the end of the war. "We must seize this chance," Mama ultimately declared. "If we don't go now, who knows when we'll be able to go again?"

Just before dawn on the day we left, we piled into the car, an eighties American Chevrolet, burgundy colored, with cream leather seats that were wide enough to fit my brothers and me along with Mama in the back. The driver Baba hired for the trip, William, an amiable Syrian man, knew just how to ease Baba's nervousness about the border crossings. Since the war had just ended—or was ending—Baba was unsure how easy it would be for us to get into the country, even though there was no official reason as to why we would be denied. William was not worried. "Just have faith," he said. "*Inshallah*, you'll be in Beirut before you know it." The sun rose as my brothers and I dozed off, while the two men got to chatting as if they were long-lost friends.

We drove north, out of Amman, past the Scandinavian Forest and Jerash, and up to the border with Syria. Still on the first leg, I regretted wearing shorts, as Amman's dewy dawn gave way to a blistering heat and my skin stuck to the car's leather seats. I was sitting in a pool of my own sweat before we had even left Jordan. At the Syrian border crossing, we got out to stretch our legs. "I need some fresh air," Mama said, complaining about our being suffocated by William's and Baba's chain-smoking in the front. We followed William from booth to booth to get our passports inspected and saw him folding Syrian pounds into the front page of the top passport to speed up the process. We all used the bathroom as Mama looked on enviously, refusing to drink or eat until we got to Beirut. "You think I can use these bathrooms if I need to go? They're filthy." Once through, we skirted around Damascus, going northwest for hours along Syria's plains before reaching the Lebanese border and driving into the Beqaa Valley.

Having grown up hearing about it, I was full of anticipation for Lebanon. I looked out the window, taking in a lushness that put our Scandinavian Forest to shame. The mountains, green and foggy, stretched out into the distance. Taking in, also, scenes of war that were gradually appearing on the roads as we drove over the mountain range and began our descent into Beirut. Craters dotting the lanes and chunks of debris piled next to near-collapsed buildings. As we drove into Beirut, urban wounds were everywhere, so fresh that the scattered concrete and twisted metal might as well have been smoldering. A devastated city that was somehow alive, teeming with traffic and people and scooters. The city itself was manic, and as we neared Tata Marcel's house, some of that energy made its way into the car. I could feel Baba wanting to speed up our arrival. Mama was agitating to get out of the car. We drove down al-Hamra, which, from the window, promised to be everything Mama had described.

Outside my grandmother's house, William had to squeeze the wide car into a tight alley so we could park just outside the building's front gate. We spilled out and heard my grandmother's familiar voice shout down from the third floor. We looked up to see her flailing her hands, greeting us, waving, blowing kisses, her ample bosom hanging over the railing. "He's on his way down, he's on his way down," she shouted. "Come up, come up." Having waited a decade to see us, the last few seconds apart were unbearable. As we waited for her doorman to come down and help us with the luggage, my fingers traced the bullet holes sprayed around the entrance, re-creating battle scenes that must have erupted on her street. *She never left*, I thought to myself as we made our way up to her flat. Tata Marcel emerged like an apparition from her front door, a character from stories we had heard. "حبيب قلبي" she wept, as she hugged each of us, and then Baba, again and again, crying into his shoulders. He kissed her forehead. "رجعت، رجعت" he whispered to her over and over again. "I've returned."

That same day, to give Tata and Baba time to catch up, we roamed throughout al-Hamra with Mama, and quickly realized she had underplayed the chaos of the street, filled with cafés, bookshops, clothing stores, and a boiling energy that was unlike anything I had experienced. Even devastated by the war, Beirut was alive, and over the coming days, I understood what my parents yearned for, being stuck in Amman. The grittiness of the streets; the crush of bodies on sidewalks; the brazenness of its people; these elements morphed into a sensory assault that left me feeling awakened, as if from a long nap.

I walked into bookstore after bookstore—most of which were nothing more than small door-sized holes in the sides of buildings. They were filled with shelves that stretched from floor to ceiling, spilling over with books that were piled in no apparent order, squeezed into every available gap. The small spaces were suffused with the smell of old paper mixed with exhaust fumes from mopeds and cigarette smoke from shop owners who were invariably sitting in plastic chairs, puffing away in Beirut's stifling humidity. I was intoxicated, spending hours making my way through titles in the kids' section, and occasionally moving on to other sections, overwhelmed by all there was to read, humbled by how little I knew.

A day or two after we got there, we walked from Tata Marcel's flat down to Bliss Street, only fifteen minutes away, to visit AUB. Laith, Nadim, and I could barely contain our excitement. We were stepping into history, into the making of our parents' relationship. We were getting to see the site of all the stories we had grown up hearing. At the main gate, Mama explained to the security guard that she and Baba were alums of the university. We left our IDs at the entrance and walked in. My parents stopped dead in their tracks. Just inside the gate, in the university's front courtyard, was a mountain of rubble several stories high. This is where College Hall and its famous watchtower had once stood, the backdrop to the picture of my parents we had seen. The rubble where the bomb had been detonated was cordoned off by tape. Students and faculty walked around it, as if oblivious to its presence. A scene of utter destruction set against the background of a sparkling sea.

II

14

IN the picture pulled out of the yellow box, now pinned above my desk, we are dressed in our school uniforms. There is a small shrub to his left and ivy crawling up the wall to my right. Our clothes are wrinkled. To hide my weight, I am wearing an oversized white shirt that hangs far too loosely on my body, he a slim black T-shirt, in violation of our dress code. His golden cross is hanging out of his neckline; mine is, I know, tucked underneath my shirt. He has his arm behind me; mine is resting over his shoulders. I can just about make out the black band of the watch I used to own on my wrist. Typically, I have a pained grimace on my face, he has his smirk. He had scribbled a note on the back.

> *Maybe one day our children will discuss this picture. They will go around saying 3ammo Ramzi the player is fingering the lawyer. I have no other picture for us. But it makes no difference; with you or with me, it's all the same. Good luck to you, this year and always. Hope we won't go back to similar situations. Love you, forever. Yours truly, R.M.*

Alongside the text, he had drawn a doodle of a man fingering another, in case I misunderstood his note. The sketch makes me smile even as a buried but familiar sensation of wrongdoing rises in my chest. Guilt that I had disappointed him in those situations to which he refers. I have no way of recalling exactly which one he might have meant. My eyes turn, instead, to the picture itself, washed out, taken as it was against the limestone wall of our school building a few years after we met.

◆ ◆ ◆

One Friday morning, shortly after we moved, Mama came down to the basement, where I was reading, to tell me that Ramzi's mom had called and arranged for him to visit. When she said his name in full, my chest tightened. Mustapha Aboud's friend. The darting shadows were being let into my home. I objected, telling Mama I would rather he did not visit, that we had not met before. She looked at me with confused eyes. "You've already met, you silly boy," she laughed. "When you were little, they lived near us. His mom and I used to put you two on the sitting room floor to play with each other for hours. You loved pretending to be farm animals!" Ramzi's father had become a renowned businessman when we were toddlers, she explained, and his family had moved to this area years ago, putting an end to our playdates. The parents had drifted apart, but recently, the moms had reconnected and discovered they were neighbors. This history, which I could not remember, offered no comfort.

He walked into my house that same afternoon bemused, as if he had witnessed a scene of great hilarity in the few minutes it had taken him to come over. He entered the basement like he owned the place, saying something or other about how cool the setup was, before making his way straight to the red and black punching bag that Laith had hung in the corner. I stayed on the beanbag, my book facedown on my lap, and watched him swing fists. Without turning around, he asked what I was reading. *The Thorn Birds*, I replied, not bothering to elaborate or to tell him of my obsession with Father Bricassart. He asked where we had moved from, where my brothers were, what we liked doing. I answered—al-Abdali, playing outside, all kinds of things—offering nothing beyond the necessary information as my eyes trailed after him.

Coolly, he walked to the Ping-Pong table and picked up the paddles, throwing one over to me. I set my book aside and got up. I had been practicing with Laith and Nadim and had a good hand. I fetched the ball and served, a low shot that skimmed the top of the net, catching him off guard. "Shit," he yelped, hitting it back far too forcefully. It shot across the room. He looked at me and raised one eyebrow. I smiled, enjoying his surprise, and offered for him to serve instead. He did, a clumsy opening shot I easily hit back. All his high arches and slow balls I refined. He followed my lead and was soon picking up the motions. We were barely speaking, the basement still, apart from the sound of the ball ping-ponging on wood and occasionally the tiled floor. He slammed his paddle once, in exasperation, when I again sent a curveball his way, the noise reverberating across the room. I startled; he apologized. "You're really good," he mumbled by way of explanation, as if that was the most unexpected thing. I did not respond, my body flushed with pride. We resumed our playful silence. After some time, the light started to turn, and shadows lengthened across the table, making it hard to see the ball. He had to head home for dinner anyway, he said, and asked if I wanted to walk him there—"to see where I live."

On that first walk in the alleys between our homes, we took the most straightforward route. Out the front door, we turned left and walked past the empty plot of land where a neighborhood mosque was being built. ("Great," Baba had said when they broke ground shortly after we moved. "We'll be woken up at 4 a.m. every day." Mama rolled her eyes. "As if anything could wake you up.") Second right and about three hundred meters down the road, we got to the intersection where his house sat on the southeast corner: a villa with a purple bougainvillea that was blooming wildly that spring. Once we got to his gate, he threw me a casual fist bump and I awkwardly reciprocated. He smiled, his dimples making an appearance as he turned to go inside. I stood there for a minute or two before walking back in the early dusk.

The streets were wider than those in al-Abdali, and cypress trees were planted on the sidewalks, forcing me to walk on the road. Streetlamps had just come on. I got to our street and looked ahead toward our home, which had a small balcony on the second floor. A weeping willow soaring higher than our house spilled its branches onto the balcony, transforming it into a treehouse. Baba sat out there, listening to his radio. Mama would join him soon with her book. It took me fifteen minutes to get from Ramzi's front door to mine.

This is fleeting, I recall thinking. I had never envisioned that someone like him, from Mustapha's world, could look kindly at me, without pity or repulsion. But then he came to say hi to me at school the next day. I was standing on the second landing, halfway down the stairs by the blue railings, unable to face the rest of the descent. I was munching on my cucumber-soaked pita, waiting for the bell to ring, *The Thorn*

Birds again in my lap. "Must be a good book," he said. "Your nose is always in it." I nodded, figuring he was on his way to the playground. Instead, he pulled himself up and sat on the ledge next to me. He put his sunglasses on and looked around, talking about something, nothing, speaking to me as if we had been doing this for years. He stopped by the day after, too. When Mustapha came over to say hi, he looked me in the eyes, nodded, before putting his arm across Ramzi's shoulder, turning him around, pulling him away from where we were sitting. Mustapha whispered, Ramzi laughed. My ears throbbed, picturing the hideous truths Mustapha was telling him about me. But then Ramzi turned to me and winked.

15

"MY fighters," Baba called my brothers and me every time we gathered around him, whether on my parents' bed while they flicked through the papers or out on the balcony, where he lost himself in thought well into the night. "I'm running ideas through my mind," he would tell us. He would contemplate work challenges and assess family affairs, make financial decisions, and play out tactical maneuvers to close this or that deal. His mind whirred tirelessly, and often, he would interrupt conversations with a question that bore no connection to the present moment, revealing that his mind was constantly elsewhere, navigating possibilities to expand and protect his kingdom.

He invited us, his fighters, to prod and challenge. *What if this happened and that did not?* He took our sparring seriously; we were all equal, from Nadim at barely seven, to Laith, who was about to graduate high school, and me in between. We were collectively engaged in shaping our future and had to play on his terms; to be logical, unemotional, and, if successful, our pushback would indeed alter his mind. Never was there a sense, however, that this democratic fraternity dissolved hierarchy. We revered Baba, and this grounded our interactions with him, even at their most informal. We saw his wisdom as formidable, and if decisions failed to make sense to us, we still trusted blindly, because there was a vast reservoir of love that underpinned his pragmatism.

As he held court, his contentment at having his three boys around him was unmissable. "I am raising tough men," he would declare, "men who know when to fight and when to stand back. Never to pick fights or prey on the weak. But to protect what is right: one's beliefs and the honor of one's family." Early on, bookishness absolved me of manliness. "He's too smart for that kind of behavior," Baba started saying at some point, speaking just as proudly as he did of Laith's fistfights, which became bloodier and more frequent in high school. "Why can't you be more like your brother?" he even asked Laith once.

Nadim and I run into my parents' room. I jump onto the bed and steady my breath, open the paper in front of my face, and stare at it as the text blurs. Nadim, dressed in his pajamas, hides behind the door. We can hear Baba's footsteps approaching, and I am trying hard not to giggle. Nadim is failing miserably. I glance from behind the paper and see him crouched on the floor, his hand covering his mouth, his whole body shaking.

"What are you doing reading my papers?" Baba asks, playfully upset.

"Boo!" Nadim shouts prematurely, jumping out as soon as Baba crosses into the room.

"*Aaah!*" Baba yells, pretending to have been startled as I dissolve into a fit of giggles, primarily at the thought that anything could scare Baba.

Before I know it, Nadim is on the ground, screaming; Baba is bent over, tickling him to tears, until Nadim begs for mercy. Baba lifts him up, gives him a peck on the cheek, and throws him onto the bed, crumpling all the papers. They settle down. Baba reclines next to us and picks up the *Jordan Times*. Nadim and I mimic him. A few minutes pass before I return to the same question I always ask these days.

"How were you going to class when Mama was protesting?" I blurt out, incredulous.

He grins.

"We've been over this, over and over again, Tareq."

"I know, Baba, but I want to hear the story again. Please!"

He sighs. Another act for my benefit.

"Your mother was crazy, Baba," he says in a tone both resigned and boastful. "She was constantly getting herself into trouble. Those rallies for Palestine were not going to get us anywhere."

"OK, but weren't you also angry?"

"I *was* angry, Baba. Of course I was angry. But Haifa had already been lost. What student could bring her back? Our leaders were looking out for their own interests. You think they cared about the refugees in

Lebanon or the protests on the streets? You think they cared what college students in Beirut thought? All your mother was doing was bashing her head against a brick wall. It was causing trouble for nothing. But she had fire within her, Baba, what can I say? She had fire within her. There was nothing she could do about that."

A protest had erupted during their student days at AUB, near the green expanse of the Oval, in the corridor connecting it to the main gate of the university on Bliss Street—the same one we entered on our first trip there after the war. A major artery of the campus, this was where all the student organizing took place, one of the few places where political activity could happen in the city without the army intervening. "This campus is considered American land," Baba had explained, "so protests took place here all the time." The corridor walls were covered with layer upon layer of posters, calls to action, leaflets, statements, student declarations, political manifestos. Some protests had to do with domestic politics; others with university affairs, like the tuition fees that students were struggling to meet; still others with regional politics. During the war, students mobilized around Palestine, especially when Israeli bombs landed in the south. Before that particular protest, tensions had been simmering on campus for days, and everyone knew that an eruption was inevitable.

"It effervesced," Baba says, "unplanned. It escalated so rapidly that the Lebanese army had to be called in. I was walking up from the business school, which as you saw is further down, closer to the sea, and I heard all that shouting. I could not believe it; I had never seen anything like that before. Uniformed and heavily armed soldiers swarming in through the main gate and into the courtyard, their batons out and ready. They were not meant to be there, you know? They were not allowed on campus. My heart sank. I just knew that your mom was going to get hurt."

On the far end of the corridor, Baba looked over the heads of his fellow students, searching for her as the troops circled them. He shoved his way through; some students were standing listlessly, others had their fists in the air, shouting. There was so much noise that he could not make out what was being said on the loudspeakers. But when he got close enough, he saw her standing on a podium, in the middle of the corridor, shouting through a megaphone. *Of course*, he thought to himself. *Of course she's the one with the megaphone.* The soldiers moved in.

"Within seconds," Baba recounts, "I saw them surround that rally and begin beating the protesters. Rima kept going, as if she did not notice the soldiers coming in closer. How could she not? She saw them. I'm telling you, Baba, she saw them, and she made the decision to stay put, not to run away. I was so angry at her. How irresponsible could she be?! They were closing in, the protesters were scattering, people started screaming. And she just kept going. Kept going until one of them, ابن الكلب, got to the edge of the podium where she was speaking, grabbed her leg, and dragged her down. She kicked and screamed and pushed and shoved like a madwoman. Not once backing down. That's when I realized, Baba, that she had been waiting for them to come for her. Waiting for them to grab her. She finally had someone to beat up, finally had a landing spot for all her rage. Baba, I thought *she* would kill *them*, not the other way round! And then she was on the floor. Boots rained on her as she crawled into a ball under their feet and made herself smaller. I ran. Baba, I ran like my legs were flying aboveground, shoving people to the floor around me. I don't know how I got to her; there were so many arms and legs flailing about. So much chaos. I got to her and pulled her out, somehow. Pulled her out. She did not even want to be pulled out, your crazy mother. I had to drag her out of there."

I shake my head as he finishes speaking, marveling at this story.

"Then what happened?" I prompt, knowing full well how it ended.

"Well, I got her out," he sighs. "But an army officer caught me. Grabbed on to my leg and pulled me back. One body for another. They beat me up and threw me in a jail cell with eighteen other protesters that night."

"You were in jail?" Nadim asks, engrossed in the story, too.

"I was. Just for the night. My head was killing me, and all I could think of was your mother, and how I was going to strangle her the next day for landing me there!" He laughs suddenly and lunges at Nadim, tickling him again.

We go back to reading the papers spread out on their bed. After some minutes, he interrupts the silence.

"I was looking out for her, Baba," he mutters, his eyes on the paper. "I had her back. But for what? She got beaten up for what?"

16

THE yard was tense. Ramzi was nowhere to be seen and I assumed he had decided to join the football game. Since our first stroll in the neighborhood, we had spent almost every recess together on the landing, which was no longer—for me, at least—a midway station to the playground. In very little time, it had become my destination; I clung to him, my indebtedness growing with each passing minute as my life materially changed. Mustapha Aboud retreated, leaving me in peace with my books or otherwise in Ramzi's company. I did not resent that I needed him for this relief. I was, rather, awestruck, amazed at how he commanded respect, how boys deferred to him, how he held himself around them. And I waited for the prank. *Why else would he be willing to, unprompted, spend his time with me?* I fretted that his friendship might one day be rescinded. He might wake up and realize his mistake. I practiced nonchalance, assumed an air of self-righteousness, acting unimpressed with everything he said and did, even as I placed myself next to him as often as I could.

With him absent, a familiar discomfort arose. I stood on the landing above the playground, feeling naked. Prior to him, I had known how to shrink myself into invisibility. But I had grown reliant on him to act as armor. I gripped the blue railings as my eyes scanned the area. The map of children around the playground was usually chaotic. But that day, a group of boys marched purposefully toward the crisscrossed metal fence in the far corner, beyond the football pitch. All the signs that a طوشة was about to break out were there. The playground even sounded different; a strange hush replaced the shouts and laughter. Boys and girls separated, a transparent divide rising between them. I looked for my brothers, who were nowhere to be seen, and then noticed that Ramzi was walking at the front of the pack. *I should have guessed*. I ran toward Maya for information, which she unfailingly had at her disposal.

"What's happening?"

"I'm not sure," she answered, her tone suffused with intrigue and drama. "I think someone cursed Ramzi's sister."

"For what?"

"Who knows? She was hanging out with Talal in that corner there."

I turned to where she pointed. Ramzi, flanked by others, including Mustapha Aboud, was walking up to Talal, who was a year older than us and more heavily built. Talal's friends were falling in formation behind him. *I should join Ramzi*. Even though it had never been spoken aloud, I knew that is what honor dictated of me. Instead of Mustapha Aboud, I was the one who needed to be at the front if I wanted to earn his friendship. Otherwise, he would see that he had been wasting his time. He would see what all the other kids, what Mustapha Aboud, could see: that I was a coward. This was my chance to prove to him otherwise, to vindicate what he saw in me—or what I hoped he saw.

I remained frozen in place.

"Come," Maya said, grabbing my hand, "let's go."

She pulled me in the direction of the fight, which I normally would have avoided. We snaked our way through the kids until we had a clear line of sight. His sister, one year our junior, had backed away from Talal and was standing on the side, surrounded by her girlfriends, pleading with Ramzi to calm down. Her words landed ineffectively as he walked right up to Talal and shoved him against the metal fence. I was close enough to see the spit fly out of his mouth as he fired a torrent of swear words at Talal. "What were you doing with my sister?" he shouted. "Relax, Ramzi," Talal said, his palms facing outward from his chest. "Nothing happened. You have to calm down. We were just talking." A vein that ran through the center of Ramzi's forehead looked like it was about to burst. It was strange seeing him like this, his pretty face a mask of rage. But it was also oddly recognizable, a face that was finally morphing to hold the raw anger that I, even after only a little time, suspected rested within him, beneath his banter and machismo. A look, also, that I had seen time and again plastered onto the faces of the men around me: Baba, Laith, others.

Talal, his hands up in defense, tried to slow down the assault. "Calm down, Ramzi, calm down," he kept repeating. "It's not what you think." He was being rational, trying to avoid a fight, but Ramzi was too far gone. Even I could see that. He pushed him again, into the fence, one time too many. A familiar scene ensued. They both inflated their chests and rolled back their shoulders. Words became grunts. The two of them collided, bones against bones, fists to jaws, kicks to stomachs. The scuffles were raw, fingers clutching at eyes or nostrils. They looked like they were stuck in a lovers' embrace. Others joined in. I was meant to. I knew that I was meant to. My feet refused to move. I could not will my body to act as his did, to be swept up in the urge I felt to defend—myself, him. I remained frozen by Maya's side, watching, my heart drumming against my chest as blood poured out of his nose. At last, boys grasped at their backs, pulling each of them away. Ramzi resisted, squirming to break free, drawn to the other, wanting to strike another blow like his life depended on it. Someone who should have been me began whispering in his ear, calming him down, placating him. It seemed to work, and finally, enough boys were able to separate them. From the corner of my eye, I could see the principal running toward us, her large hairdo flapping against her forehead.

The mania in the courtyard defused as instantly as it had erupted. Ramzi turned and walked through the crowd, which parted to make room. Boys rested their arms across his shoulders, whispering in his ears. Someone passed a tissue to him, which he stuck in his nose, bloodstains streaking down the front of his white shirt. His sister was sobbing in the corner. The whole scene barely lasted a few minutes, but it was mesmerizing; I could never act the way he did. This is why he was friends with Mustapha Aboud. They had his back at times like these. I turned to Maya, who shook her head. "Boys are idiots," she said. I laughed uncomfortably, because I knew that, idiots or not, I had just witnessed Ramzi being the man Baba told us we needed to be. Fighters who stood up for one's honor, like Baba pulling Mama out of an angry horde. Or like Mama, even. I had no fire. I was a set of slumped shoulders at the bottom of the staircase, holding on to the blue railings. I feared I had lost him. Then, as he walked past me, his face beginning to swell, he put out his fist. I gave it a bump, shaking my head, pretending to disapprove while filled with nothing but reverence.

17

كس اخت هالبلد—Ramzi said one night as soon as they were out of earshot.

We were sitting on a pavement that was more cracked than whole, Amman's orange and pink tiles uneven and broken. We had spent the evening like we did most nights, meandering around our neighborhood, deciding where to sleep, his room or mine, a custom that began weeks into our friendship. Unable to make up our minds, we settled in a nearby alley, between two olive trees and against a crumbling stone wall. I feared its crevices were filled with cockroaches. The ground was littered with dirt, dry leaves, and fallen branches. Fruit that had not been plucked lay burst open, trodden by cars and feet, rotting in the heat. Stray cats congregated at the end of the road, lazing around metal bins and rummaging through the trash, collecting flies. With no cars around, we could hear the crickets. The jasmine bushes in the garden behind us peeked through the olive branches and over the wall we were leaning against, their fragrance assertive and pungent.

The final echoes of the muezzin's dusk prayer hung in the air. The sky was beginning to turn. Just down the road, under the bright green light of the minaret, the mosque's congregants spilled out into the street. We watched them for a few minutes before he spat his words out with a venom that startled me.

"Fuck this place, man. This whole town should be burned to ashes. What a backward nation."

"*Ssssh*," I hissed, worried that the women walking past might hear him.

I had grown accustomed to his outbursts. This time he was irritated by the smattering of men and women returning from prayers—their conservative attire, the women's hijabs, the men's one-toed leather sandals. His tone betrayed a conviction we all had, but never said out loud: We were superior to them. People like us, like our families, we were more enlightened. We were not enslaved by our religion in the same way. The masses huddled on floors in mosques; their numbers made their faith, their lifestyle, too common for our liking, unrefined and vulgar. Our Christianity, which we donned in symbols—golden crosses hanging on thick chains around our necks or from the rearview mirrors of our cars—loudly proclaimed we were not them, assured us that we were more civilized.

I picked up a small pebble from the side of the road and rolled it around in my hand, resting my chin on my knees. I was uneasy, he could tell, but I had not learned how to hold my thoughts in his presence. He reached into his pocket and pulled out his Marlboro Reds, a habit he began when we were barely fifteen. He offered me one, jokingly, knowing that I balked every time. It was the hypocrisy that rattled him, he went on, the performance of conservatism. Tightly wound hijabs in public hiding wanton lust and depravity in private. It was a conservatism that we were all forced to abide by.

"*Our* lives are confined, made narrower," he explained, "because of *their* small-mindedness. We'll always be a backward nation, man. How can we not be when this is how they live their lives and how they force us to live ours?" he said, pointing to their retreating backs, shaking his head.

He leaned into his lighter, the reddish glow of the flame illuminating his handsome face. His head was shaved closely to his scalp. My eyes traced the fine veins that snaked down his temple and pictured the thick vein that ran down the middle of his forehead, the one I had first noticed in the schoolyard. He inhaled deeply and held his breath in for a second or two, like he always did, his tongue flicking over his lips, savoring the residue of smoke in his mouth. The burning orange of the cigarette's ember floated between us as dusk turned to night. I watched him blow the smoke out of his nostrils, my body relaxing as the tension in his eased.

In our jasmine cocoon, sheltered as it was from the city's tyranny, he assumed his throne with confidence. Unencumbered by having to perform for anyone, he set his mask aside, letting me peer in. He grumbled that our roads had become parking lots for the local mosque every Friday at lunchtime, when the entire neighborhood drove in for noon prayers. Complained that our country was falling apart because of pathetic and uninspiring leaders. Held in contempt the smallness of our people, who went around proclaiming obedience to king and God, like hamsters on a wheel. Mocked the children in the playground, forgetting he was one of them, for their macho behavior, their zealous masculinity, their territoriality around this girl or that one, their constant struggle to preserve an honor that appeared irreparably fragile.

I listened, amazed by the ease with which he lived. The way he existed in our world even as he railed against it. Thrived within the same confines he ridiculed. I could barely break through the authoritarianism with which I policed my own thoughts, let alone conquer and mock it. Instead, I was enthralled by him even as my life split in two. Time apart from him meant time to hear my thoughts, to sink into a whirlpool of confusion where answers could not be had. Endless prayers marked the hours we weren't together. My voice soothed me under showers, where no one could hear. *Shampoo. Condition. Hot water blasting. Soapy water washing away the disgust. Scrub harder. I will pray for forgiveness before I go to bed.* Next to him, I found relief, my internal monologue quieted. Out there, people talked, *3eib* loomed ever-present. The darting shadows terrorized me. Absolution remained out of reach despite my bruised knees. With him, in our alleyways, I could breathe.

"Fuck this country and its people who don't forgive, man," he was saying, reading my mind. He leaned in and nudged me with his shoulder, snapping me out of my melancholy. "And fuck this habit," he smirked, pointing to the cigarettes. "I have to quit. This summer. And to join the gym, too," he finished as he blew the smoke out.

I gave him an admonishing look, having heard all this before. The street was dead quiet—as still and unsurprising as the white city around it. I was thankful for the predictability of our evenings. We never bored of making plans that failed to materialize, the joy resting solely in their making. Goals that helped us push back against Amman's aimless days. Darkness gathered. The ember of his cigarette moved back and forth to his mouth. I listened, barely speaking, hoping that one day I, too, might stop performing. That I, too, might take away my mask, and reveal to him an inner self. That one day, he might listen, once I figured out what it was that I had to say.

◆ ◆ ◆

The truth is, in his diatribes, Ramzi was only mimicking the adults around us, who had much to be stifled by in their host city, where what little they could enjoy of life unfolded behind closed doors. Every Thursday evening, one set of parents would host a dinner at their place, as the same group of friends—from school, from church—rotated between people's living rooms. With a handful of restaurants and very little to do in Amman, our lives were reduced to the interiors of our homes. They were an odd clique. With most having been forced into Amman from elsewhere, our families all remained tethered to where we had come from. Perhaps because of that, we all had a peculiar manner of relating to the space around us, perpetually holding ourselves apart from it, never responsible for it.

My parents remained captivated by the Lebanon of the seventies, and when they hosted, the conversation turned nostalgic. Lebanon was like a foghorn, resounding through their present, reminding them of how far they were from the utopia of their past. Baba went around telling everyone that this place we had landed in was—comparatively and objectively—a backwater. "Look, look," my father would often proclaim in astonishment, "look how that man is leering at the woman. Her shorts barely go down to her knees! In Beirut, women can walk down the street in a bikini and no one blinks." Truth was beside the point. Battles raged over women's bodies, modesty in Amman a sign of backwardness, nakedness in Beirut a symbol of modernization.

Beirut knew nothing of the restrictions that shackled our families in Amman. The city was unapologetic, with a voracious appetite for living that was rooted in its fragility. Nothing could be taken for granted, and one day did not naturally lead to the next. The city kept up a dizzying pursuit of hedonistic bliss while, in the background, the crucial matters that made life mundane, that ensured its continuity, fell to the wayside. Our white city was settled in its predictability. A reserved and self-conscious younger sibling to Beirut's sophisticated and worldly older sister. This was a discrepancy our parents never failed to point out as they romanticized Beirut's openness against Amman's stuffiness, forgetting that the deathly spiral of the former had forced them to seek life in the latter.

18

IN the mid-nineties, Palestine beckoned to Mama. The intifada had given way to peace talks and the promise of a Palestinian state alongside Israel. "It's about time," Baba proclaimed. "This is the best we'll get." Mama disagreed, but, although suspicious, she was willing to put up with the rhetoric of peace if it meant she could visit. She had only been once, when she was thirteen. Tata's diary marks that trip minimally: *April 1967: We visited al-Quds, Ramallah, Jericho, Hebron, and the Jordan River. This is the first time I visit Jerusalem since 1948.* Just short of two decades after they had landed on Lebanese shores, Tata and Jiddo had traveled with Mama and Khalo from Beirut to Amman, and from there, driven the two hours to Jerusalem. This was before Israel's occupation of the West Bank and the Gaza Strip had begun, and Palestinians were still able to visit some of their lands.

"What was it like?" I asked Mama as I watched her pack for this trip.

"The only thing I remember is getting catcalled in the Old City in Jerusalem," she giggled. "It was hardly an auspicious trip."

Less than two months after their visit, the June 1967 war changed everything, as Israel expanded its occupation over whatever had remained of Palestine after 1948, severing it from the region around it. The drive Mama's family had gone on became instantly unimaginable. So, when the possibility of doing the trip presented itself in the mid-nineties, Mama's curiosity got the better of her.

"I want to see what has become of the place," she told Baba, making it sound like she was checking out the renovation of a friend's flat. "I will just pinch my nose," she said, "and go," referring to the odious expectation that, to visit our homes, we must recognize those who stole them. Far from perfect, far from just, this was the best we could hope for then, she said, and she was going to find Tata's home in Haifa. Baba tried to convince her to wait, to see how the dust might settle around the talks. But she was adamant, refusing to budge despite his pleading, replaying a past dynamic between them that had been submerged in Amman; her fiery political commitment and impulse to confront, his aversion to challenging power and acquiescence to the status quo. As he must have done so often during their Beirut years, before Amman had domesticated her and tipped their dynamic in his favor, he relented.

This idea of return that Mama kept talking about—that refugees must return—Tata could not understand. *Return to what? The Zionists had decimated Palestine; it was gone. We had no family left there. Who would she see? Where would she stay? What was there to return to?*

The whole time Mama was absent, Tata was restless, walking around the house, whispering her prayers, talking to herself.

"يا ربي" she mumbled throughout the day as she sat around in her floral nightgown. "How fortunate our family has been, fleeing unscathed, time and again. Look how we ended up. We should count our blessings. We thank you, our Jesus, for looking out for us. We're all together and in good health, حمدلله. Please continue watching over us. Please bring my daughter back safe."

Then, a few minutes later, "God works in mysterious ways."

Tata could not fathom how Rima had traveled to Palestine, how she was in Haifa, looking for the home from which she herself had fled close to five decades earlier. Tata's life had been neatly compartmentalized by geography. A childhood in Palestine; a marriage in Lebanon; a matriarchy in Jordan. These compartments were disconnected and impossible to reconcile. The first two had ended in blood. The third she was holding on to with all her might. Yet here was her baby girl, doing the impossible. She was going back, as if undoing all that time had done, as if undoing flight.

"I have seen hate in their eyes, my son," she told me. "I have seen it. These people will not stand for a Palestinian woman like your mother, one who does not know how to keep her mouth shut, one who will tell them what she really thinks. They kill, they kill, they kill, and they get away with it. They kill and somehow it is our fault. Why would they not harm her? What is one more dead Palestinian to them? Nothing. We do not even register. May God open their hearts and end their blindness and hate."

The language of peace had never entered Tata's vocabulary.

Then the call came. Mama was ready to come back. As surprised as Baba was that Rima was ready to finish her trip after five days—far sooner than the ten days she had planned—he was relieved. He went to pick her up from the central bus station in al-Abdali, where buses from the Allenby Bridge drop off those who cross over from the West Bank into Jordan, and as soon as she walked out of the car, Tata rushed toward her, hugging and kissing her as if she had not seen her for years, blessing her and offering her gratitude to Jesus.

"OK, OK, Eva, OK, OK. حبيبتي امي, I'm back, you have nothing to worry about. I'm back. You can relax now."

Around the dinner table, this time, Mama spoke without interruptions.

"All of it is there," she started. "All of it is there, and none of it is there. I don't know how to explain it. It is as if Palestine is there, but she has become European. It's not ours anymore. You feel like you're walking in Paris or London. The streets are sparkling, the grass is lush. Haifa looks like a European capital on the Mediterranean."

She talked about the Old City in Jerusalem, about Wadi al-Nisnas and the Bahá'í temple in Haifa. She roamed the streets, taking it all in, wanting to inhale as much of it as she could. "I knew, I knew from day one that I was never going back," she said, and this was her chance. She went to Akka and saw the kids jumping off the piers into the water below. She walked in Jaffa and visited the old markets. Then she turned to Tata.

"I couldn't find it, امي. I looked, I followed your directions. I just could not find it."

Tata nodded.

"معلش يا بنتي," she said. "The important thing is that you are back in one piece. What does it matter if you found the house or not? Either way, it's no longer our home."

Mama nodded.

"I could not stay one second longer," she explained. "From the day I went into the embassy here to get my visa, the whole experience has been demeaning. I can now tell you the truth. It has all been humiliating. That I would need their permission to go to my home—such arrogance. Even while there, feeling their gaze on me, seeing what they have done with the place. It pained me. We would have never been able to do that. They know what these lands, our lands, are worth. Look at what we've done to Beirut. If Haifa had stayed with us, we would have destroyed her, too. But then, I don't know. It's all there. But it's also gone. It's beautiful, it really is. It's just not the Palestine we know anymore."

19

WE are sitting in eighth-grade English class, my legs stretched out in front of me, the top of my thighs scraping the bottom of my desk. The wooden surface is carved with messages of love, swear words, and an array of initials long enough to rival the school's official records. I am in the front row, next to Maya, Issa behind us. Ramzi is in the last row. This is the class after recess, and he had been looking forward to it the whole time we were in the playground. Our teacher walks in, more made up than usual. Her hair, dyed a flaming red, is straightened and pulled into a ponytail that rests high on her head. She is wearing a tight-fitting black top that shows off her ample cleavage, a red skirt that goes with her polished nails, and white sneakers.

"Today, we are reading *Macbeth*," she tells us, as the sound of pages turning fills the room.

Halfway through class, Issa taps my shoulder. Miss Fatima has her back to us, writing on the board. I turn around and he passes me an envelope. This one has Scotch tape on its side; a folded A4 sheet taped into the shape of an envelope with *TB* written on its front, the initials highlighted with yellow marker. I recognize Ramzi's handwriting, as he has taken to sending me scribbled notes in class. But this is a step up from the torn pieces of paper that usually land on my desk, crumpled and messy.

Inside is another folded A4 sheet. I pull this out and straighten it on top of my open textbook. The portrait he has drawn is titled فاطمة المفقودة. It takes me some seconds, three or four, to make sense of the crowded pencil sketch, and when I do, panic rises in my stomach. I sense Maya looking over my shoulder and I immediately shove the paper in my pocket, my face flushed. I turn around, frowning. He is giggling so hard it looks like he's about to keel over. The paper burns through my gray trousers, radiating heat against my leg. *There is no way*

I am going to get away with this. I am livid with him for putting me in this position. *I will throw this out as soon as the bell rings.*

Miss Fatima *is* beautiful. But that is not why he has a crush on her. "She knows things," he told me in the playground, right before class started. He had leaned in close when he said this, close enough for me to smell the fragrance he must have sprayed on in preparation for her class. He was almost whispering, his tone shifting, deepening, as he invoked her name. He sounded conspiratorial, as if he had stumbled onto a secret that he wanted to pass on to me. "What things?" I asked, more nervous than curious about what he was going to divulge. "You can just tell she is really good in bed," he said, deadpan. I was confused. "What do you mean? How could you possibly tell that?" I hoped he would not hear the crack in my voice, the desperation of wanting to know more. He shrugged. "I can just tell." We sat in silence, my mind buzzing, his submerged in lustful fantasies. "You'll see," he said, swinging himself off the ledge as soon as the bell rang. "I'll be fucking her before this year is through."

"Yes, Ramzi," Miss Fatima's voice punctures my thoughts, and I turn around, wide-eyed, wondering what other trick he has up his sleeve. He smirks and, holding my gaze, asks her if he can go to the bathroom, "to take care of some business."

"I don't need to know anything about your business," she answers, "but yes, you may go."

Then she smiles. She smiles! I am watching this exchange and I see in her smile what he means. He rests his hand on my shoulder and gives it a squeeze as he walks past me and out of the classroom. *I told you.* He leaves, the class resumes, the portrait burns in my pocket.

The day stretches but I can hardly concentrate. When I finally get home, I dump my bags and head straight to the bathroom. I take the envelope out and try to decipher the orgy of limbs stenciled in pencil. Five—maybe five and a half—naked figures, are sketched out, although it is hard to tell for certain, given the intricacies of the body parts flailing about. What is not hard to discern is Miss Fatima, smack in the center of the drawing, straddling a man with eight-pack abs. The man, I assume, is Ramzi. She has her hair tied up, like she did in class, and a choker on her neck. A word bubble drawn from her lips says, "دلعوني دلعوني." The man underneath her is saying, "اخ... كلي خرة يا شلقة." The various lovers all have bubbles with an imaginative array of expressions. Hanging on Fatima's breast is a three-dicked creature sucking at her nipple. Helpfully, Ramzi has an arrow pointing at it that says *ALIEN*. Fatima has apparently been abducted into an orgy in this fantasy he has sketched out.

Sitting on the bathroom floor, I shake my head and smile. *He's insane.* I want to dismiss him, but I can't. I am drawn to his world, to what he is sharing with me, craving to be a part of it, to inhabit it. I know this is my brothers' world, and that it was Baba's before them. I, too, want a part in it. But I suspect my own cartoonish fantasies can never be stenciled, sketched, or shared. I iron the wrinkles out and put the paper back into its homemade envelope. I place this letter next to all the other notes in my bedside table; torn pieces of paper and random Post-its he had passed on to me at school fill the back of my drawer. Something has changed. I consider hiding the growing stack in a more private place where Mama won't see it.

20

THE color was light, somewhere between purple and blue, so faint it was almost white. Paint buckets lay by our feet, along with brushes, large and small. We were cramped in my room, him, me, and Musa, who had transferred over from the all-boys school to join our year as we entered high school. As a newcomer, I included him often in our activities. This time: painting my room. We had just pulled the furniture away from the walls and covered everything with old linens. Piles of books were spilling off my bed. "When do you have time to read all these, T?" Ramzi asked. He took charge, explaining that we had to sand uneven surfaces on the walls for the paint to spread evenly.

We began. The mood was jovial, as it normally was when the three of us got together. Ramzi and Musa had quickly grown fond of each other and were mischievous in a way I was not with either. Standing in the middle of the room, over buckets of paint, Ramzi mocked Musa crudely, asking how he was adjusting to the abundance of girls in our school. *Would he rather fuck this one or that one? Did he prefer this one's ass or that one's tits?* His mask was on. Teenage lust and machismo followed by pitches of giggles.

"Ya, man, we can put her between us, on all fours, her head here," Musa was saying, pointing to his crotch, "and her ass there," pointing to Ramzi's.

"Argh." Ramzi rolled his head back, acting out what he thought it must feel like to slide into this imagined body as he thrust his hip forward over the row of buckets arranged between his legs.

I leaned into the wall, sanding, feigning disinterest despite all their attempts to get me involved. "Come on, T, don't you want to get in on the fun? You can stand right here, take turns," Musa said, pointing to his right. "Yes!" Ramzi shouted, humping the air and high-fiving Musa over the space between them. I shook my head and muttered something or other about how silly they were being. My mask was on, too, and it was one Ramzi had become familiar with. *You are above this childish banter*, he had written in one of his letters. *People in Amman don't appreciate you nor your goodness.* Like Baba, he believed the alternative reality I projected, seizing upon bookishness and faith to explain my behavior.

Up and down I sanded until my arms began to ache. The room filled with dry, scratching noises as the two of them resumed their work with vigor, energized by what they had just shared. Grateful for a break, I walked to the window, opening it farther. The normally cool interior was made sticky with the three of us sweating in close quarters. It was not even noon and the stench in the room was thick. I stood at a distance from them, to catch my breath and to shelter myself from this nameless sensation taking root in my gut.

Dreams of *Sayida Mil'aqa* and games with my cousin had been only the beginning. I glanced back at Ramzi, lost in his sanding duties, sprinkles of white dust settling on his sweaty forehead. His button nose. The scar above his eye. The curious contradictions he embodied. Aloofness offset by friendly dimples. Petite features that projected masculinity. I wanted to hold his face, to feel his body, to see how it might respond to my touch. Getting him hard; what power that would entail, to mechanically produce that kind of transformation. That faceless body between him and Musa, that's who I wanted to be. *I want to be his plaything.* The creature whose sole purpose was to bring him pleasure. A vessel, an empty shell. *Transform me!* my body was saying. *Make me as good as you are.* Or just: *Make me.*

I walked to the center of the room and put the sandpaper down.

"You done sanding already?" Ramzi asked.

"Yeah, I think so."

Absent-mindedly, I dunked a large paintbrush into the bucket and moved it to the wall, splashing dots of paint all over the plastic sheets we had spread at our feet. I began rolling the brush up and down along the wall's length, evening out the paint. There was something else as well, a more innocent feeling. I wanted to partake in his play. His freedom in acting the way that he did with Musa, without fear of eliciting mockery, was as foreign to me as his lust toward the girls at school or his fistfights in the playground. An emancipation of the body—mine was rigid and controlled, every sinew alert, primed to deflect unwanted attention. Musa shared a language with him that, even back then, I knew I could not access. Ramzi's mask made him stronger, mine made it hard to breathe.

More giggles from the two of them behind me and I consoled myself that there was no need to be part of their routine. There were other times when I stood on the inside next to Ramzi, in a space that was ours alone, that were more meaningful than the show the two of them put on. There was relief in that thought, and to prove my point, I reminded myself that I was sleeping at his place that night while the paint dried in my room.

We strolled through the neighborhood to get some fresh air before heading to his house. After Musa's departure, we fell back into our rhythms, our gaze solely on each other—him no longer performing; me, listening, containing him, trying to find myself in his words. My entire body ached and the muscles in my shoulders throbbed from the long day. I was ready to call it a night, but I knew he was delaying our return to his place and another tense moment with his dad, who was on his case about everything. His grades, which were average. His smoking, which was well above average. His drinking, which never went unnoticed. His father set a high bar. The eldest child and the only son, Ramzi was—in his father's eyes—a pillar of the family, the protector of his younger sister, a man of the house. His expectations hardened the more Ramzi rebelled, and the more he expected, the less Ramzi delivered. He was stuck in the vision of manhood his father demanded; I never deluded anyone that I could live up to that ideal and was spared the expectation. That is perhaps why he turned to me often, with guilt, with frustration, unloading during our walks or in letters that landed in my backpack or on my bed. Letters that were becoming lengthier, more introspective, more frequent. Letters that needed to be written but not necessarily read, with me acting as little more than the custodian of his thoughts, the witness to the rebuttals he lobbed back at his father.

Two loops around our block before we made it to his home. We walked into the kitchen, where his dad, with his green eyes and hairy belly hanging out of his unbuttoned shirt and over his boxers, was working over the stove, preparing dinner. Unlike Baba, his father loved to cook. His mom, relieved of her domestic chores, looked relaxed in her pink post-siesta nightgown, smoking a cigarette, watching the news. His younger sister was doing homework in the back garden, waiting for the meal to be served. Ramzi's frustration was incongruent with the energy in his home, which was light, without an electric current running through the air—as it did in mine—or none that I could feel, anyway.

"That paint better have dried," his dad said with mock sternness, his Syrian accent making him sound perpetually witty. "Dinner is almost ready. Set the table," he said, waving the spatula behind his back.

Ramzi's sister bounded in as he and I spread out plastic sheets on the chairs so we could sit down.

"Can I join tomorrow?" his sister asked, eager to spend the day painting with us.

"Nope," Ramzi responded.

"Nothing to join," his father interjected as he placed pots on the table. "He's staying in to study tomorrow."

Ramzi looked at me and wiggled his eyebrows upward. *We'll see about that.* I shook my head as his father turned to me.

"Are you ever going to help this one get similar grades to yours?" he asked me.

"That's an impossible task, 3ammo," I chuckled, throwing Ramzi a guilty look.

"Well, one can hope," he said, before sitting down to say grace.

Ramzi and I turned in soon after dinner, him in his bed, me on the mattress on the floor right next to it. His room was mostly dark. Faint rays of light seeped in through the blinds from the garden lamp. As was often the case when I was stretched out next to Ramzi, the night promised to be a sleepless one. The air was oppressive, pinning me down. I was unusually aware that the windows and door were shut, and that I was locked into this cubic space with him in a way that was in equal measure arousing and claustrophobic, especially as the day's exchanges lingered. He was annoyed at his father, and I wanted to comfort him. The proximity of our bodies was no longer benign, and in the stillness before dozing off, I was tormented by how close we were. *I could slide into bed with him. Hold him. Maybe even say something funny and clever, coded, that would invite flirtation. Run my hand on the inside of his thigh.*

"I'm horny." His words punctured the space between us.

I knew all the reasons I should recycle a wisecrack Musa might say, something in jest that would compel him to move on. I did not.

"Oh, yeah? Show me."

He swept the covers off his body. I sat up and looked over. His cock was hard, its tip peeking through the elastic band of his gray-blue boxers. The sound of deep quiet was punctured only by his steady breath. The bedcovers under my hand were soft. I could still smell the faint residue of paint on him. I looked at his body and was in that sacred space again: private, dark rooms, where I felt powerful. I expected him to put the cover back down. He did not.

What were you doing? What did you want from me?

Instead of asking, I obliged and leaned in. His dick glistened, a drop of pre-cum oozed onto his tummy. I wanted to see more closely, to lick that moistness, to take him into my mouth. In that moment, in lust, Ramzi's presence was immaterial, just as Khalo's had been, to my own desires. This was between me and his body. I hovered for barely a few seconds, even as my memory recalls a period longer than that, and the moment was gone in a flash. He lowered the covers. His seduction, or invitation, or curiosity, or whatever that was, remained fleeting. I leaned back as my dick pulsed in my own shorts. No sooner had I reclined into my mattress than the bedroom door swung open, and light from the outside corridor flooded over us. His dad popped his head in and cheerfully asked if we needed anything before he turned in. I croaked a *no* as I closed my eyes and offered my gratitude to God for his protection.

21

IT is hard to figure out, exactly, where envy ends and infatuation begins. Almost immediately, after that afternoon Ramzi waltzed into my basement, I became consumed by his presence, his way of being, his wit and confidence, the absence of doubt in his head, his ability to command rooms and people. Those features became the blueprint for my own happiness. If only I could become him, someone who was better and manlier and handsomer and stronger. Who he was defined who I needed to be to belong in our white city. And I wanted—more than anything—to belong. I looked at him with insatiable envy—not the ill-wishing kind, but the one full of hunger and desperation. I wanted what he had because what he had was good and recognized and affirmed. What I had—what I was—needed to be erased. Yet the more like him I tried to be, the more of myself I relinquished. Amman embraced him as it pummeled me. It reminded me of what was objectively true.

He was the boy I could never be, or, as we grew older, be with.

22

IT was late when he called and asked me to come over. He sounded funny; his voice strained. "I need to talk," he said. Mama was in bed and Baba, as was his wont, was watching TV late into the night. I snuck out. The neighborhood was asleep, a dog barked nearby, no cars drove past. *I wish we had agreed to go for a walk instead*, I thought as I let myself in through the glass foyer at the front entrance to his home. I stood by the vase filled with peacock feathers, studied my reflection in the mirror, then tapped softly. He opened the door and pressed his finger against his lips as he led me to the salon at the back, where his parents entertained guests, where we never sat. The sound of TV streamed down from the floor above.

He went behind the bar. "Do you want a drink?" he asked as he poured himself a whiskey. "Won't your father notice?" He shrugged. "He knows, and anyway, they're already pissed off with me." I declined and sat down. With burgundy sofas and dim lighting, the room presented itself warmly in shades of red and brown. "Why are your parents pissed with you?" His cigarette packet was on the table, three stubs in the ashtray. "You know why. I'm just a jerk. I have not studied in weeks, and he knows it." He took a sip. "There is nothing they won't give me, طلباتي الهم اوامر. And I can't even focus to study, to give them that in return." He pulled a cigarette out, leaned into the lighter. "How's the math O-level treating you?" He blew smoke out, smirking. "Easier than the chemistry, right?"

We competed in math; where I studied hard, he was naturally gifted and often had to guide me along. "Yes, sure," I chuckled. "You know, I can help you with yours if you're struggling." He laughed, nodded, and we fell into a silence unlike past ones. He was forlorn, far from me. I waited, unsure what this was about. "You'll do really well in the exams, because you deserve it," he said. I gave him a perplexed look. "You do, too." He shook his head. "No. No I don't. I'm not like you." I asked what he meant by that. He ignored me, pretending not to hear. He took another drag, hovered the cigarette's tip just above the ashtray as he exhaled, holding it there, watching it, before he tapped the ash out. "You seemed to have a great week," he said suddenly. "Maybe it was because I wasn't around you." The words landed with a thud between us. The colors of the room took on a threatening shade. Again, I asked what he meant by that. Again, he ignored me and kept going, reciting words he had clearly rehearsed.

"Tanya was there all the time," he said. "That girl has no idea what a special person she has in her life." His words slurred. He had been drinking long before I got there. The formal setting he had ushered us into for this confrontation now made sense. "Ramzi," I said, forcefully, fearfully, "what are you talking about? Are you upset with me?" We had not hung out together for a few days, since that weekend we had painted my room. Earlier, a school friend, Tanya, and I had sat on the steps next to the football pitch, where he was playing, talking about nothing in particular, joking about this or that, watching him play. At one point, I looked up, and our eyes—his and mine—met across the yard. I must say, part of me understood, even back then.

"Tanya is the only person on this planet I would die for," he blurted out, reading my mind. "I love her." My insides churned. "I'm sorry I haven't told you this. I just don't know how to be close to her. Should I ask to be her boyfriend? She'd say no. Should I put my feelings aside and become, like, her friend? Like you?" His eyes bore into mine, demanding answers. I had none. None he would want to hear, anyway. None I could articulate. "Maybe you should tell her how you feel," I whispered, wanting to give him something, anything, to stop him looking at me. To distract myself from the questions his questions had unleashed. We were speaking around the unspoken, beginning to give it form, definition. Tanya's presence clarifying boundaries that had until then remained unrecognized. The beating in my chest drowned out the noise from the TV upstairs. Although I knew I shouldn't, I pushed for answers. "Ramzi, you want to tell me what's going on?"

"Nothing," he said. "Nothing is going on. I just get scary thoughts sometimes, get confused. I wonder what more I could be doing for the people in my life, everyone who I'm letting down." He knocked back his glass. "You're not letting anyone down," I interjected. He shook his head. "No, I'm irresponsible and selfish." He got up and poured himself some more whiskey. "I'm your opposite in every way. You're good. I'm just not. And I am tired, Tareq, a lot more than you can imagine. I am fed up with the world, bored with this life and with living." The room was smoky. It was late, later than I had thought, and I wanted to end this, to not be around him anymore. His tone scared me. I could not bear watching him like this, and I was apprehensive—that he might see me, or I him. "You should go to bed," I said, lifting myself to the edge of the couch. "You've had too much to drink and you're not making any sense."

"No, no, I don't want you to go. And I don't want to go to bed. I'm trying to tell you something," he hissed. "Tell me, then," I shot back, "because I'm not sure what all this is about." He looked up from his whiskey tumbler. "Two things. I want to tell you two things. One, you mean a lot to me. Please never doubt that, even when you see me acting like a three-year-old. And two," he continued, "take care of Tanya for me. Be with her when I can't be. Make her laugh when I can't. حطها عشاني بعيونك." His voice cracked, my breath caught, the pain in my chest sharp, unavoidable. I got up and walked around the coffee table, crossing the schism starting to open between us, and took him in my arms, where he molded himself against my body. He rested his head on my shoulder and—for the only time I had ever known him to do that—started crying. I held him, patting his back, stroking his scalp, calming myself. "Snot," he said finally. "I've covered you in snot."

23

I INVITED him to the Dead Sea, where my family was spending the Easter holiday that year. It would do us good, I thought, to be in a different space. My parents did not object; he had become an extension of our unit. I was giddy, for the lake and its surroundings, and more privately, for the prospect of sharing a hotel room with him. We had spent countless nights in the same room, but a hotel was thrilling, a blank canvas. Filtered light and lifeless hills marked our steep descent into the Jordan Valley. Forty-five minutes south of Amman, we were in the depths of the earth, an unworldly place; pressurized, hot, stupor-inducing. Our sense of time altered. Everything slowed down, and within hours, we were all sluggish, nourished by the air, marveling as our skin was turned to silk by the salts in the water. Days dissolved in the heat, and come nighttime, we were drained. Wakefulness next to him gave way to deep sleep.

On our last day, we were in the lake, floating cross-legged. Uncharacteristically peaceful, I stretched out on my back on the surface of the water and bobbed up and down in the current, waves lapping at my neck and ears and rays warming my tummy. Golden circles swam behind my eyelids as I dozed off. It must have been only a few minutes later that I sat up. I had drifted a good way from where Ramzi, my parents, and my brothers were floating. I looked back. All their attention was fixed on him. Mama's laughter carried over to my ears. My brothers were on either side of him. Baba was listening so intently that he did not notice my drift. He was fearful of the Dead Sea and its notorious currents and would normally have called me to move closer.

I can see the sun's gold on the waters between us, the hotel in the background the only sign of life. All around, barren mountains and a haze in the horizon where Palestine lay, barely detectable. A thought burst into my mind, at once strangely familiar and utterly threatening in its foreignness. A sensation that had long been known but had remained unformed. *He fit into my family.* Effortlessly floating in the lake, the saltiness of the water tickled the back of my throat. He had crossed into the private realm of our lives; Mama and Baba had let their guard down, no longer performing civility around him, and my brothers had long thought him a better match than me. *He fits.*

I squinted, looking at him all bathed in sunlight, as this thought crystallized in my mind. *I hadn't invited him along as my friend.* The sulfuric water added to the claustrophobia closing in. I sat up abruptly—too abruptly—my arms and legs jerking ungracefully, and the next wave, although gentle, tipped me over, splashing salty water all over my face. I closed my eyes against the familiar sting. *I love you.* Sour water landed in my mouth. I gagged—the dense waters of this dead sea made it hard to breathe. I needed to get to shore, to splash fresh water over my burning face, but with my eyes firmly shut against the sting, I had no idea in which direction I needed to swim.

That night, everyone retreated to their rooms after dinner. Ramzi and I decided we should mark our final evening with an ارجيلة and snuck out to a hidden alcove slightly removed from the beach. He ordered his تفاحتين, the burning coals the waiter placed between us only marginally hotter than the nighttime air. We sank into our seats, revived, exhausted, barely speaking, the only sound between us that of the bubbles rising in the pipe. Clouds of smoke infused with the tobacco's sweet fragrance washed over us with every exhalation. I watched him smoke; how he rested the plastic tip of the pipe lightly on his lower lip and held it there, occasionally closing his mouth around it to inhale, too relaxed to move the pipe back and forth.

"You seem withdrawn," he said.

"I do?"

"You do. Is there anything you want to tell me?"

"No, I don't think so. Just trying to figure out some stuff."

He nodded, satisfied.

"You'll tell me when you're ready?"

"Yes," I promised, "I will. I'll tell you when I'm ready."

Lightheaded, we made our way back to the room just after midnight.

"I want to run a bath. Did you see how big that tub was?" he said as we ambled back.

"Sure. Go for it."

I sat on the bed in our air-conditioned room and flicked through channels, trying to ignore the sound of water running behind the closed bathroom door. I pictured him standing in his boxers, inspecting his tan lines in the mirror as water filled the tub. Lanky arms and hairy legs. Small paunch with the thick trail leading into the elastic band of his shorts. The shower of hairs across his chest. Shaved head, reddened from the day's sun. The water stopped, I could hear him step into the tub. I looked at the television screen, the sound of him settling into the bubbles. Then the occasional splash. I could hardly breathe.

"Baconi! Come in here!"

I froze, willing myself not to move.

"Baconi!"

"يلى يلى. I'm coming," I whispered.

I slid off the bed and walked toward the bathroom. He had left the door unlocked. I opened it and stood face-to-face with a wall-sized mirror above the sink. In its lower right corner, his small head was crowned with foam. He had given himself a mustache, a beard, and bubble hair, and was staring straight at me with his grin and childish pride.

My nonchalance usually materialized without thought or effort. A casual shrug or the performance of exasperated impatience. That night, my reflexes diminished. Perhaps it was the extent to which submerged desires had surfaced over the course of the day. Or the general exhaustion of maintaining a charade despite everything within my being rebelling against it. Or maybe it was the sun and the salt that had strengthened me. Or the residue of the three words that had floated through my mind merely a few hours previously. My denial was cracking.

Standing on that marble floor, the continued performance of indifference sapped all the energy from my body. I was underwater, gliding with great effort toward him, sitting on the edge of the tub, as if it didn't fire up all my nerves to do so. I put my hand in and barely registered the water's warmth. We spoke about something or other. My hand brushed against his thigh. The pull was gravitational.

24

I HAVE no idea when I left that bathroom or how I slept that night, and no memory of our drive back to Amman the following day. Sitting on the edge of that tub, all I had wanted to do was get into the water with him, touch his face, and wipe the bubbles out of his eyes. I went to church that first Sunday back. Tata and I had begun attending Mass, next to our house, run by a young, handsome priest in his midthirties. She found his sermons energetic and kind, less stale than those delivered by the older priests in Amman's main churches. This church was small, sparsely decorated, as if imploring congregants not to be swept up by grandeur, but to focus on the Lord instead. The cross by the altar, two bits of wood joined together, was even less adorned than the one from Jerusalem hanging over Tata's bed. I sat next to Tata for a bit before kneeling in the space reserved in the front of each pew for prayer, my knees resting on a red cushion that was still wrapped in its plastic cover.

I prayed for absolution. This time, there was no subsequent calm to be had. That night, I turned to that space that Ramzi and I had cultivated over the years. I wrote him a letter that is in my safekeeping, here in the yellow box. He must have handed it back to me at some point. I pull it out.

I walked into church this morning and felt a lump in my throat. Everything that I have been trying to ignore came back to me and I was overwhelmed. I am a complete failure. I really screwed up. Memories came into my mind and I saw them in a different light. I felt hollow and fake. I do not know why. I can explain none of this. It was as if I have betrayed every person around me and I hated myself for not being worthy of their trust. I sat there and I prayed and prayed until I thought I had repented. But these things in my life are irreparable, and there is no real salvation from them.... For all 17 years of my life now, I have held and kept everything as well as I know how. Today, I wanted to let go. I did not. I remained hanging in there, even though I discovered how much of a failure I am. I know that God will give me a second chance. He will not desert me, and I will not let Him down.

A few days later, I found an envelope on my bed.

To Tareq Baconi, House no. 55,
تحت دعارة أم عاطف بجانب النخبة للأراجيل الشعبية

What the hell was that about? You have seen nothing of real life. When you get older, you'll look back at these days and laugh knowing you have much bigger things to worry about. You're still 17, man! Fuck Amman. Fuck Amman on a dinosaur's dick. Fuck Amman's people for making us suffer all their bullshit. But God is merciful and knows his followers.
   Keep the faith, man. I'm here. I'll always be around. RM.

I read that line over and over, comforted by its assuredness and frightened by my need for it. *I'll always be around.* Ramzi is right, I thought. *Fuck Amman. Fuck Amman on a dinosaur's dick.*

25

IN the summer of 2000, life stretched ahead of us, unknown and intriguing. I had one year of high school left, after which I was to go to AUB to follow in my parents', and Laith's, footsteps. Ramzi was leaving school to go to university. We both pushed off the impending change, as every day became a determined but ultimately futile effort to hold on to what was already fading. The city, until then claustrophobic and confining, became precious, filled with experiences we wanted to capture, to hold on to. "For the last time," we kept saying. *Let's go to Frosti's ice cream in Shmeisani, for the last time! Let's go to Chilli House for the coneys, for the last time! Let's go to Falafel al-Quds in the first circle, for the last time! And shawarma al-Reem by the side of the road, on the third circle, for the last time!*

We spilled out into the city with every opportunity we got, hardly spending time indoors. Each morning, he came to pick me up in his mother's beat-up Volvo, proud of having acquired his driver's license before any of us, using some واسطة or other. Even his honking had a singalong tune. I rushed down the minute I heard it, dressed in my swimsuit and tank top, my tennis racket slung across my back, ready for a day by the pool at the Royal Automobile Club, which my parents had decided to join as Baba's business flourished. The sun was blazing-hot even in the early morning, the car toasty, windows all down, air rushing in. Amr Diab was big then, and he blasted out of the speakers as Ramzi drove us like a madman down Amman's eight circles toward the club.

"Slow down, slow down!" I shouted. "You're going to get us killed."

"Relax, man, just chill. You're literally the only one in Amman who wears a seatbelt," he laughed as he leaned over and unbuckled the belt.

I sweated nervously the first time we drove up to the gate. A guard was standing outside his one-person cabin, bored with life, holding sheets of paper to cross-reference the names of club members. High walls loomed over the entrance, topped with broken glass to prevent people swinging over.

"Just play it cool," Ramzi said. "He'll have no idea that I don't have a membership. Don't be awkward."

I shot him a look, regretful as he inched the car toward the guard.

"صباحو" Ramzi beamed. "How are you this morning?"

The guard nodded, flashing the look of utter disdain and contempt that is standard Amman.

"هلا" he answered gruffly as he put his hand in through the window for our cards.

Ramzi handed him Laith's ID, which he had placed in his wallet, and my own. The guard squinted at both cards as I fidgeted with my seatbelt, safely buckled back in. Ramzi looked at me, winked, and leaned into the back seat to get his Marlboro Reds from his backpack. He put one in his mouth and pulled another halfway out, before extending the packet toward the guard. He looked at Ramzi, back at the cards, then nodded and took the cigarette, leaning into Ramzi's lighter.

"يسلمو" he mumbled, waving us both in.

And that was that. He drove through, looked at me, and chuckled.

"You worry too much, bro, you should learn from your older brother and just take it easy," he laughed as he squeezed my thigh. "Life is only as hard as you make it out to be."

Every morning, that whole summer, Ramzi flashed my brother's ID and sweet-talked the guard, who never inspected our cards again. By the end of August, Ramzi was asking him about his family, how his children were doing, how he was coping with Amman's skyrocketing living costs. I sat beside him, as quiet and marginal as I usually was in his presence, confident that had I been the person exchanging pleasantries with the guard that first day, we would never have gained entry. That was just the way he existed in this world—with ease, with lightness, everything opening up to him without his trying. Every morning, we drove up the winding driveway and ambled toward the pool, where we lounged, read, drank, made evening plans. Later, a barbecue in my backyard, or argileh at Tche Tche's, or saj sandwiches around Abdoun Circle with Maya and Musa.

Time acquired a strange quality that summer. It stretched endlessly, each day seeping into the next, expanding, with us frozen in place, unmoving, living each day exactly as the one before. Yet we were also being hurtled forward, toward a rupture we all sensed was coming. The city was in step with us, oscillating between its typical stillness, its boring predictability, and the transformation beginning to flood its streets. Western names we had only become familiar with during holidays abroad or through American sitcoms were materializing around us. Food chains were the first ones in. Hard Rock Café and Planet Hollywood both opened in Abdoun, and every day brought announcements of new brands and outlet stores, restaurants and shopping malls.

There was mania when McDonald's and Burger King christened their flagship drive-throughs. People lined up the night before. *Finally*, Ammanis were saying, *we've joined civilization*. Ramzi, too, wanted to stuff his face with a Big Mac. We sat in the car one night, closer to dawn than midnight. He was in the driver's seat, drunk, having driven us back from a house party despite all my protestations. Fries and burgers were spread out between us. He was playing *Jagged Little Pill* on repeat. I was fighting off the melancholy that I fell prey to frequently that summer. "This Big Mac tastes different," he joked, his mouth full. I looked at him, cocked my head for an answer. "It's halal," he blurted out, laughing so hard at his own joke that food flew out onto the windshield.

We loved going to Books@Café in the first circle. This place, too, was one of the early signs that Amman was breaking out of its confinement. An internet café, when most of our houses still did not have a dial-up connection, attached to a bookstore with a massive backyard that spilled over the edge of the first circle toward downtown. The view of East Amman from the café's terrace was spectacular: homes, densely packed, carpeting the hills of the city, punctured with the emerald green of minarets. A view that well-to-do West Ammanis loved to look at but never venture into.

"This place has the best argileh," Ramzi and I told everyone, which was an absolute lie. He went because Tanya had started working there for the summer as a waitress. I went because he did, but also because a faint curiosity was forming in my mind. Books@Café was gay-friendly, a known but unspoken fact that somehow materialized in our consciousness without ever being acknowledged or affirmed. A venue that was out of time and place with its surroundings and that, like its gay founder, lived in a liminal space common in Amman, where one is simultaneously seen and unseen.

We sat ourselves there as often as we could, on the cushions sprinkled throughout the backyard, propped up on the slope looking eastward. Amman's evening chill against our sun-soaked skin made us shiver, and we wrapped ourselves with the blankets lying around. He was fixated on Tanya, who was shy, made more so by his observing her every move. She was the only person who made him lose his cool. In her presence he was clumsy. Her soft demeanor was difficult for him to navigate; this boy who was energetic and present and big, losing his footing. It was as if in her stillness, she could see behind the image he presented to the world, and he found that both alluring and intimidating. His infatuation developed into a friendship that flirted with romance as we held court those evenings. People came and went, saying hello, sitting down for a smoke. It was there that friends gifted me the yellow box for my birthday, filling it with candy and decorating its inside lid with glitter and paint. And it was there that he, Tanya, and I lurched into a triangle of the most predictable sort.

Ramzi's passion for Tanya was all-consuming. He envisioned his love as the brightest of flames, one that might devour him in its intensity. She was not to be sullied in the same way as other girls, and never came up in his playfulness with other boys. His love could not be diluted into lust; it was closer to idolization. To be a man worthy of her love, he was to protect her honor, to safeguard it. Against her fragile femininity, he projected a possessive masculinity. She was his, and he placed her on a pedestal, beyond bodily desire. He spoke daily of wanting to be worthy of her. She, like me, presented an image of goodness that he felt entirely lacking in his own life.

Where his love for Tanya was undefiled, almost asexual, mine for him was depraved. The more boys around me were vocal about girls, the wilder my fantasies became. Without any outlet in the daytime, my mind exploded in darkness. Sleepless nights filled with episodes as real as any wakeful moment. As he moved closer to Tanya, every fiber of my body pulled me closer to him. I jerked off thinking of him, then immediately banished those thoughts. Recited prayers as I tried manically to tame my mind.

We were both obsessed—his obsession with her becoming fodder for my obsession with him. But never once did it occur to me that my infatuation might in any way resemble his. My love was not only unworthy of being requited, it was unworthy of being admitted. I never once imagined competing with Tanya for his affection. Quite the opposite; I knew Tanya brought him joy. I wanted him joyous, passionate, blissful, aroused, even if none of those emotions in him could ever conceivably be directed at me. I wanted to bring Tanya closer to him, as I fantasized of pulling him closer to me. And I knew that, like Books@Café, the existence of my desire was conditional, permitted only if it stayed within the realm of the unspoken.

That summer, Amman was on the cusp of maturing from a village where everyone knew everyone else's business to a place none of us could quite yet describe. We, too, were on the precipice of transformation, but we comforted ourselves that much of our lives would remain the same. Even with Ramzi at university, I would still see him regularly, to study together or walk around the neighborhood. Our days were as intertwined as they had always been, and nothing was going to change that. But now, thinking back to those sunny days, I'm not sure why we both kept saying that everything we were doing was *for the last time.*

26

THE summer ended with Ramzi going to university and me returning to school. We kept up our strolls, but gone were the endless hours hanging out in the courtyard. To make up for the time we no longer shared, our letters became more frequent. They flew between our homes; we popped them under each other's pillows or stuffed them into jacket pockets. Sitting in London, I peer into the yellow box that became the hiding place for the bundle of letters that I had, until then, kept in my bedside table. I re-create our exchanges, sift through his side of the correspondence, imagine what I must have written to elicit this or that response, reconnect with the young boy in the photograph hanging next to my desk.

Tanya became the most precious part of him I could hold on to, the conduit through which we explored the limits of our friendship, the boundaries of our intimacy. To keep him close, I moved closer to her. Assumed the duty he charged me with. She took his spot by the blue railings, sitting next to me every recess. Without him, neither of us was sure how to be. We began playing cards; sometimes it would be just the two of us; other times, Maya, Musa, and Issa would join. I became possessive, manipulative, even—that much is clear from Ramzi's often-bewildered letters. *I just don't know what's going on. You and Tanya seem to be getting quite friendly. If you're falling for her, I would be the happiest person in the world, because I would know that the girl I care about is in good hands. Your hands. I want to give you the time to be with her, since that makes her happy.* He wanted her to be happy, as I did him. I laughed off all his doubts about Tanya and me and promised to tell him what we spoke about.

In the alleyways, we talked for hours, and I guarded that time zealously. He had to tell me everything that was happening, every little detail. *That was the true measure of a friendship*—I must have written something along those lines—*confiding one's deepest secrets. When you turn to me with your thoughts on Tanya, I know that you trust me. That you've chosen me as your best friend. When you shut me out, it hurts. It is a sign that you do not trust me.* I know that this is the argument I made because that was how he framed his response—and his reluctance. *It is my secret garden with her. If I give you 2% of me, then you'd own me, little brother. I never felt comfortable talking about Tanya to anyone. I won't love you any less. You know that. I hope you do. I am independent. I do not like seeking advice. I like making my own decisions and leading my own life.*

He said these things even as he came to me often. I was the one who shut him out, frightened as I was about his instincts to exclude me from that secret garden, desperate to cultivate our own. I pulled away and began spending time with Musa. *You've been acting real weird lately, and I have no idea why. Musa slept over at your house twice last week,* Ramzi wrote after I had passed on our walks for a few days in a row. *I feel like a stranger around you. Fuck you. When did I last make you feel so unwelcome?* His jealousy affirmed me. Assured me that he, too, was possessive. That he, too, had grown fond of our time together and was worried about my planned departure to AUB that fall. *You mean the world to me,* he wrote. *You do. Let us get over this thing that has been bugging us for too, too, long, and start over. After all, I only have a few more months with the only brother I have ever known. Don't fail me.*

❖ ❖ ❖

From the yellow box, I pull out another letter from that tumultuous period. Each time my eyes scan it, they see an alternative future that might have been, had I been braver, had I known then what I know now.

You said today that you are not angry with me, but you are disappointed with the situation. How can you be disappointed when you know I am here for you and when you know I am happy? How could it hurt you? Am I not being fair? Am I not giving you everything? Am I not listening to you? I think it is none of the above. So why do you feel disappointed? What is missing? Do you think I'm running away from you? Do you think I don't care? Last night you were happy. Today, you are not, it seems. Why do you always have these ups and downs? Does it have to do with me? Am I hurting you? Am I upsetting you? What? What am I doing wrong?

I am struck that disappointment is how I conveyed my pain to him. Not heartbreak, or confusion, or fear—but disappointment. Forced to submit to the silence all around me, I became untethered, and he—well, he *was* inadequate, unable to see what could not yet be seen. Creases are tearing this letter apart. I gently turn the page over.

I told you I am always there for you. You don't want that anymore? You seem like you started to hate me. You seem to have lost trust in me. You do what you think is right and what is best for you. You won't lose me, and I will always be supportive. I mean this part more than anything. You are a hell of a wonderful brother and friend. Even if you are gay, I will love you still. I am proud of your deeds and actions. I wish you the best of luck and I hope that you can deal with everything hurting you at this moment. I hope you let go and start over. Don't underestimate yourself, Baconi. Move on the way you want. No one has any right to tell you how to be. Just don't hurt anyone in the process.

Feel free to call me a little more often. When you need anything, we can go for a walk, or discuss it in FLEX while we exercise. If we join. Let me know if you need anything, but as for me, I need some time alone, to set things straight in my fucking head.

Love always and forever,
Yours truly

I ask myself if he meant what he had written, that he would love me even if I were gay. I recall the pain in my stomach where those words landed, offered through his hands, hands that I loved. Transgressing as he said the unsayable, giving my thoughts life. Charting the path for me to do the same. All I had to do was own them, write them back. Isn't that what I most wanted? But there was so much space between those words, written, and the reality I lived. I read those lines and thought to myself: *Why are you doing this, choosing an example that is so utterly horrid to demonstrate your devotion? You think that would have compelled me to speak of love?*

It was hard to believe he could ever love a part of myself I reviled. His acceptance made me despise him.

27

ONE dusk, I was stretched out on the couch in our sitting room, reading. I was alone at home, except for Baba, who was sleeping down the hall.

"Baconi, you home?" Ramzi called as he let himself in and up the stairs.

I put my book down to find him beaming. He lifted my feet and sat at the end of the couch, placing them back in his lap. He was bursting to tell me something.

"What's happening?" I asked, getting up to fetch us some water, or to pull away from the easy intimacy between us.

"I've been grooming."

I knew immediately what he was referring to. It was all he could talk about those days. The trip he and a handful of Mustapha Aboud's other friends had planned, to Aqaba or Sharm al-Sheikh, or some other nearby shore. I had not been invited. I listened to his plans with as much excitement as I could muster. There were updates: he had decided to arrange for prostitutes to come to his hotel room that weekend. "Finally," he said, "I get to practice." Hence the grooming. He thought it would be fun to shave a message for the prostitute into his pubes.

"Do you want to see what I wrote?"

Standing opposite him, I was thankful for the glass in my hand. Before I had a chance to respond, he began unbuttoning his jeans, pulled the flaps open, and looked up at me. I had become bolder with time, after our close encounters that neither of us fully understood. I took a step toward him and put the glass of water on the side table. Our eyes locked briefly, and without any hesitation, I dropped to my knees, placing both hands on his upper thighs, the fabric of his jeans rough against my palms.

Were you goading me? What the fuck do you want from me? Why are you playing with me in this way?

Rather than questions, there was only stillness, and not yet the recognition that he might have been the one doing the manipulating all along.

Our sitting room, with windows on two of the four walls, was exposed to the street below. Baba was less than ten meters away. Anyone could have walked in, like his father had done the other night I had slept over. The consequences would have been unbearable. My skin tingles writing this, knowing that we were more naïve than brave. None of that mattered. My surroundings retreated as my world shrank to the space between his legs. He lifted his shirt, exposing his love trail, and pulled the elastic band of his boxers down. His pubes had been trimmed into a stubble, and there was the faint shape of a symbol or a mark where he had shaved closer to his skin. The shadows were getting heavier, and I could not read what it said. I leaned in closer—so close I could smell fresh soap and dampness. He had just showered. One of my hands rested softly against his, helping pull down the elastic band of his boxers, my thumb gently stroking the back of it. The other reflexively reached up to trace that shaved area. Arm in midair, before my finger settled onto his skin, the reality that had receded came crashing in.

In a second, I saw how compromised I was. I looked up and our eyes locked. His smirk was gone, his mouth hung slightly open. His dimples had disappeared. His eyes bore into mine in a way I had never seen before. They were foreign, stripped of their warmth, seeing me anew, there kneeling in front of him. Lust mixed with disgust, power. Clarity. *How long had you known?* I backed up and walked to the far wall, putting distance between us, turning the light onto an altered space where strangeness had settled. Out of the intuited and into the known. The innocence of our friendship had evaporated, in seconds, morphing our love for each other into a convoluted mess of misunderstanding—or, rather, finally, of understanding.

I never did find out what symbol he had groomed, nor whether prostitutes did materialize. By the time he went to Aqaba, or Sharm al-Sheikh, a couple of weeks later, I was no longer in his life.

For a few days afterward, we limped along, navigating our way back to a friendship in which I was increasingly masochistic, him irritated. The devastating knowledge that I could never have him, let alone that I wanted to have him in the first place, settled in my chest. One day, after one such fight or other, after I had slammed the phone on some complaint he was making about my behavior, he wrote me a letter. It was late autumn, before the end of his first term at university. The letter rambles on and on, about my ups and downs, my self-flagellation, his jealousy of Tanya and me, my needing assurances, attention. Then the letter asks some questions.

Am I not being fair? he wrote. *Am I not giving you what you want? Am I not listening to you? Do you think I'm avoiding you, or that I don't care? Am I not being kind, or am I hurting you in some way I don't understand, or what? What is going on, and why do you keep trying to convince yourself that you're not good enough? One day, you'll be a king, Baconi. Move on. Move on the way you want. For both of our sakes. I'm starting a new page at 12:44 a.m. Want to come over tomorrow? I love you so much. Ramzi.*

Maybe it was the plea in this letter, the desperation. Or it was the recognition that we—I—had taken things too far, skirting around what was becoming increasingly obvious, destroying what was left between us. I was tired—tired in a way that no trip to the Dead Sea could remedy. He was a voice in my head, telling me there was goodness in me, and between us, not only ugliness. Telling me that all these fears I harbored—that I was vile, unholy—were all untrue. I held on to that voice, to pull us out of this spiral. With his letter in my hands, I stepped into a role I had been anticipating—dreading—for years. My actions were confident, assured, as if I had been here before. I was convinced that any outcome my decision could produce would be more tolerable than our slow, dreadful unraveling. Like a switch going on, I no longer had patience for unresolved questions. After years of inferences and implicit hints, of deflections and half-truths, I was overrun by urgency, by a pressing need to force acknowledgment where none had existed.

My memory of the letter I wrote to him fails me. The absence of any response to it in the yellow box makes it difficult to reconstruct. Yet some truths I recall with great clarity. Staring at a blank, white sheet of A4, placed on my pillow, against the book I had been reading. It is late, chilly, and I am stretched out under the covers. The bedside lamp is on, and I am clutching a pen, preparing to write while propped up on my elbows. I haven't even started and already my shoulders are aching in this position. The sound of the TV from the sitting room is faint, drowned out by Baba's snoring. Ramzi's letter is spread out next to the one I am writing.

My dearest Ramzi. This is how I began most of my letters to him—formally, compared to the jest in his. I imagine I was brave in the words I chose, audacious. *I have a secret to tell you.* I recall being gutsy, confessing that I was attracted to him. That is merely a suspicion, however, based on no evidence other than the ferocity of the reaction that followed. Any honesty must have been tempered by my own confusion. I wrote what I wrote, and I folded the paper. A single page. That fact I can recall with certainty. Honesty needs few words. I put the paper into an envelope and licked its flap shut. I then placed his letter and mine in the yellow box, ready to be delivered to him the next day.

An unfamiliar calm descended over me afterward. That, too, I remember. I had off-loaded my burden. I felt safe. I had put myself in his hands, the best hands. He was so perceptive, so much worldlier than I, he would help us feel our way through these strange lands. Draw a silly doodle that would turn my demons into horny aliens. Protect me like he did everything else. Tell me what I needed to hear. I turned off the bedside light. The bluish haze from the TV screen flickered through the space under my door. I fell asleep in minutes.

28

"TAREQ! Ramzi is on the phone," Mama yelled from the sitting room a day or two later.

I was seated at the table we had moved into the middle of my bedroom so we could study together. I pushed my chair back and picked up the receiver.

"Hey," I said, "I'm already studying, are you joining? Where are you?"

"My parents read your letter."

His tone was terse. He had forgotten it on his pillow, he explained. His mom had read the note. "My parents say it's best if we do not see each other anymore." He said these words rapidly, wishing to dispose of them. I would have done the same.

"It would be best if you stopped coming over."

"Tareq? I'm sorry. Look, I'm sure they'll get over this. It's just for a few days. We can talk once I'm back from the trip next week. Tareq?"

My hands were shaking so badly it took several attempts to get the receiver back into its cradle. I could still hear him pleading into it, but my mind was several thoughts ahead. There was none of the righteous fury that would have been needed to slam it down. Anger might have been a more appropriate marker for the last time we spoke. Mama. *His mom must have called mine. What do I tell her?* My knees wobbled and my T-shirt was soaked. A chill ran through my body, and I sat on the side of my bed, trying to recall the letter's content, irretrievably lost. My most private thoughts, those that had taken a lifetime to form, had slipped from my grasp. Others had read them. *Who? Who had read them? What had I said?* Others were making decisions based on them. Banishing me. Judging me. Bile flooded the back of my throat.

Mama. I got up and walked into the hallway. Mama came out of my parents' room, where she had been reading the papers with Baba. She stood outside her door and looked at me. *I was too late.* Shame seared my insides. My mask had been yanked off and she could clearly see the boy Mustapha Aboud looked on with such contempt. I remained rooted in place, outside my room. Mama walked down the hall and hugged me. The force of her touch was electric. My hands came up, to push her back, away from this repulsive body. She tightened her hug.

"What happened? Tareq, what's going on?"

"Did Ramzi's mom call you?"

"Yes, she said you had sent Ramzi a weird letter. She was worried about you and wanted to check in and see if you were OK."

"Ramzi told me she read the letter. He said I wasn't allowed to see him anymore."

"Yes, she said it's better if you don't go over for a while. Tareq, what's going on? What was in that letter?"

29

MAMA held me as words tumbled out—this time, with no preamble or manipulation of the truth on my part. Her loving assurance that nothing was insurmountable was instantly forthcoming. "We will deal with this issue, whatever it is, together." But the gravity of the situation dawned on me when, a day or two later, she suggested I speak with Baba. Not all matters make it up our family's hierarchical chain. Most are dealt with directly by Mama, often in an attempt to keep them from Baba. In any case, she was the one who had first talked to my brothers and me about sex and given us a sex-ed book that narrated the basic mechanics. With the assumed abstinence before marriage, this was not a matter that needed revisiting. But now, bringing Baba into the discussion signaled an escalation, that the issue was beyond Mama's capacity to resolve—itself a jarring proposition. "Maybe he went through something similar when he was younger," she offered, to soften the blow.

Diagnosing my predicament was a challenge. The very few stories that were known to us back then were surrounded by an aura of scandal and *3eib*. They were traded in hushed tones and behind closed doors, their articulation unsavory and compromising. A member of the royal family exiled to Canada because he was "different." A famous artist slain in his residence by a jilted male lover. Such drama did not happen to families like ours—Christian, middle-class, untouched by slander. In our city, where truths are hidden behind manicured exteriors, there was no easy prescription to be offered. So, one evening, at Mama's prompting, I put on a sweater and walked out onto the balcony.

During the week, Baba's schedule ran like clockwork. There were two windows to catch him at his most attentive. The first was just after lunch and before his siesta. Those were the periods he was at his most jovial, and when Laith, Nadim, and I would sometimes find ourselves congregated in my parents' room. The second was a few hours later, after Baba woke up but before he became consumed with work calls well into the night. Mama would bring him coffee on the balcony, where he would sit listening to the evening news while puffing on his cigar. Even when Amman was bitter cold, he would wrap himself with a camel-skin robe and stay in the frigid night, catching up on work that was stuck in a pre-digital constellation of calls, radio, and papers. When done, Baba would sit back, gaze into the distance, and, between news segments, tune his portable radio to Western oldies or Arabic classics, like Umm Kalthoum, who often serenaded him with her soliloquies. He would stay out until my brothers and I got ready for bed, after which he would head inside and, in his nocturnal way, watch TV until the early morning.

Mine was a conversation best had in the shadows. That night, like all nights, Baba had his radio balancing on the balcony's edge and the ashtray close by. A plume of smoke rose from his cigar and swirled in front of his face. His robe rested around his shoulders. With his right hand, he methodically worked his prayer beads, moving one onto the other. His reverie broke as I walked out onto the balcony.

"طروقة العظيم," he sang, using the nickname that only he ever greeted me with. "How are you, Baba? How was your day?"

"Good," I mumbled as I settled into the plastic chair at the other end of the balcony.

Without another word, Baba returned to his pseudo-meditation. It was incumbent on me to break the silence. My limbs shivered, in cold or anticipation, and my fingers tried to scrub out the black marks on the chair's otherwise pristine white. Chris de Burgh's "The Lady in Red" came on and floated to the street below. The branches of the weeping willow dangling opposite our balcony swayed in the breeze. I looked ahead, to the roofs of the houses around us and up to the clear sky. I drew a deep breath and brushed aside the self-consciousness swelling in my chest.

"Baba, I need your advice," I said abruptly.

Without missing a beat, Baba leaned forward and lowered the music. He turned to me, nodding. A seriousness descended over his features. My brothers—who had no idea what was going on—had made themselves scarce, as I would have done had I sensed one of them seeking this space with Baba. There would be no interruptions. There was no easy way to begin the conversation, not that I fully understood what the conversation entailed. The words that had tumbled out to Mama had been defanged by their articulation and were as good a starting point as any.

"I'm confused," I began. "You know Ramzi is my closest friend, has been for many years."

Baba nodded.

"Recently, I've realized I have feelings for him."

I paused. These words, out in the open, spoken, given weight. I expected an altered state, the air around me shifting. With the most incriminating confession out of the way, it was easier to continue. I recounted my story, then ours—Ramzi's and mine.

Baba looked at me, picked up his cigar from where it had been resting on the ashtray, and put it back in his mouth. He struck his match and moved the flame to the tip, puffing three or four times to light it back up, and began smoking, without any rush, as he looked ahead. Every few minutes, a car would pass down our street, its engine interrupting the quiet.

"Baba, I wouldn't worry about it," he said, as if nothing out of the ordinary had just transpired.

His tone was mellow, unperturbed. A rush of excitement ran through me.

"You mean this is normal?" I asked, fearful that I might jeopardize this promise of salvation by hoping for it.

"Of course it's normal. You're young. We all have urges at your age. Boys, girls. It doesn't matter. Don't worry. It's just a phase—you'll grow out of it."

"So, this happened to you?"

"Yes! It happens to everyone. You remember my friend Hikmat in Paris?" I nodded. "He and I were like brothers, like you and Ramzi. I went through a phase of feeling attracted to him. You have hormones swimming all over your body. You get turned on by trees at your age," he chuckled.

"But, Baba, I'm not attracted to girls. I'm only attracted to boys." I was desperate not to underplay my admission or to inadequately explain the nature of my sin.

"Look, Baba, don't think about it too much. It will pass. Just ignore those feelings. When the time is right, a girl will catch your eye. I promise."

The door to the balcony swung open and Mama walked out. She shot me a tentative look as she walked to Baba's side and placed a plate of cut and salted cucumbers in front of him.

"Baba thinks it's just a phase," I offered, bringing her into the conversation.

"Yes?" she asked, her voice, too, betraying hope.

"Of course it is. Don't put other ideas in his head. We all go through this," Baba said, sensing that behind the scenes there had been a more dramatic exchange.

"I was thinking of taking him to a therapist to help him talk about these things."

"I don't think he needs a therapist. But I guess it won't hurt." He turned to me. "Baba, you've always been the brightest kid in your class. Your mind is powerful and sharp, and you think like I do. You let ideas run with you. That's a good thing. But you need to learn to control your mind, to bend it to your will, not the other way round. Don't let your thoughts control who you are. Your mind is a scary place if left to its own devices."

Less than a week later, I was in the car with Mama. A rainy day, gray and wet, with a chill that is peculiar to Amman's desert winters.

"Zip up," Mama cautioned, easing the car to the side of the road and stopping opposite the dreary-looking building.

She put the hazard lights on as the cars behind us honked. We had agreed it was best for me to go in alone. Garden Street's unforgiving traffic and the angry cars blaring their horns behind us left no room for doubts to surface.

"I'll be here in an hour and a half," Mama said. "I'm just going to do some shopping and will pick you up when you're done. It's on the third floor. Dr. Dajjani. Zip up! You'll get a cold."

I stepped out of the car and watched her merge into traffic. She did it Amman style, nudging the car's hood one inch at a time out of her slot until she forced the cars behind her to brake. I stepped into the five-lane traffic in the three-lane highway alongside other pedestrians spilling off the sidewalk and crossed to the building Mama had pointed out. Dr. Dajjani's clinic was housed in a seventies residential apartment block that had been converted into health-care facilities. The gray skies made the building look more forlorn than it otherwise might have. I scanned the black-and-white placards at the entrance and spotted Dr. Dajjani's name. "Psychologist, Third floor." Degrees from a number of universities were listed under her name, preemptively answering any challenge to her authority.

The staircase was dark and dank. The floor needed a good mopping, as did the elevator, an old contraption with shiny silver surfaces that disfigured my reflection. I knocked on the clinic door and a young receptionist, head covered in a hijab, buzzed me in. There was no one in the waiting room. I checked in and took a seat. Simple wooden chairs with faded pillowcases were arranged around a low table covered with piles of Arabic newspapers and *National Geographic* magazines. The space was lit with cold fluorescent lighting that, against the worn furniture, made the room oddly welcoming. It reminded me of Jalileh's apartment. I flicked through a *National Geographic* magazine, looking at the pictures, unable to commit to reading an article, too distracted by the receptionist answering calls and giving directions to the clinic.

"Tareq, the doctor is ready for you."

I got up, knocked, and walked in. Dr. Dajjani was sitting behind a desk at the far side, facing the door. She stood up and met me halfway. She shook my hand and gestured for me to sit on one of the chairs arranged on the other side of her desk. She was nothing like I had imagined her. A middle-aged woman with kind eyes, light brown hair tied into a bun, and large reading glasses dangling on her chest. Meeting her put me at ease; it did not seem outrageous that I would be telling her about Ramzi. She finished scribbling on her notepad before turning to me.

"Have you been waiting long?" she asked, smiling.

"Not really."

"Good. Good. Why don't we start with you telling me a few things about yourself? How old are you?"

"Seventeen."

"And which school do you go to?"

"The National Orthodox School."

"Ah, lovely. And you're now finishing your A-levels or توجيهي?"

"A-levels."

"Excellent. Have you figured out where you're going next?"

"AUB in Beirut. That's where my parents want me to go. That's where they went, and my older brother is studying there now."

"OK, good," she said. "So. Tell me, Tareq, how can I help you today? Why have you come to see me?"

"I'm not really sure how to start."

"Just tell me whatever comes to mind. Don't worry, there's no right or wrong way to start."

For the third time in a little over a week, I spoke of Ramzi. Dr. Dajjani nodded along, but her features registered no surprise, no indication that my story was anything out of the ordinary. Perplexed, I thought perhaps there wasn't anything unusual in what I was saying after all. Perhaps this was a story she was accustomed to hearing from boys my age. Or perhaps she maintained a professional poker face no matter what she heard in this room. Mama told me that her friend had recommended her as a good therapist for children and teenagers my age. I was curious about what those kids came to her with, and just as my mind began wondering, a suspicion formed. *Had Mama briefed Dr. Dajjani on everything?* The sense of betrayal came sharp and quick. *What did Mama say? What did they talk about?* The absence of ownership over a secret that had long defined my private thoughts left me regretful at having trusted so openly. But I rapidly brushed those feelings aside. *I have no way of knowing what Mama said, if anything. I am here now and all I desire is to see this through.* Baba had urged me to control my mind, and I wanted to know how that could be done.

"Dr. Dajjani, the thing is," I ventured, "I have tried to train myself. I have tried, hard, for years. I am just not attracted to girls. I have been attracted to boys my entire life, even before I knew what I was doing."

She nodded, jotting down notes. Her soft features and calm eyes encouraged me to go on until I had said all there was to say. I stopped speaking, praying that the sincerity of my appeal might compel her to intervene.

"Look, Tareq, I want to talk to you about those dreams and the feelings of attraction you've been having. It is very easy for someone, especially a young man like yourself, to analyze certain situations inaccurately and to convince themselves of an idea that is not grounded in reality. I do not doubt that what you are saying is true. That you have dreams about boys. That you feel attracted to Ramzi. But those dreams could mean many different things. As a child, as a teenager, you may have misinterpreted their meaning and latched on to an idea in your head that is not the right one." She paused. "As men and women, Tareq, we can choose not to succumb to basic desires. We have the ability to think. This power is what separates us from animals. It is what makes us human."

She paused again, waiting for me to react.

"Tareq, what you're describing is not unusual."

"It's not?"

"No. Look, these things happen in the natural world as well. Have you ever seen a male dog climb behind another male dog?"

I shook my head.

"Well, it's not unnatural. It happens with animals. But here's the thing: When animals do it, they're not doing it to mate. What is happening is that one of the male dogs is humiliating the other, degrading him, conquering him. It's a show of strength. For humans, it's the same. It's unnatural for two men to be together in this way in the context of a sexual or emotional relationship, because it's degrading, and insulting. It is an act that destroys one's honor."

I said nothing. She carried on.

"What I'm trying to say, Tareq, is that the urge itself might not be unnatural. It is normal for people your age to be sexually overactive, and to be attracted to both men and women. Acting on it, however, is what becomes unnatural."

She waited for me to speak, but I could not utter a word.

There was nothing I wanted more than to be like my brothers or

Ramzi. Yet, even as I struggled with the depravity of my thoughts, Dr. Dajjani's words offered no solace. Even then, I knew they were not the resolution I was seeking. I clasped my hands in my lap, just out of her view over the desk, and dug my fingernails in. My trust in Mama and Baba had been premature, as it had been with Ramzi. They had no answers. In fact, the only one who had answers was me. I had been doing what I needed to be doing, until that letter. I had let my guard down, trusting Ramzi, when I should have known better.

Numbness took over. Begrudgingly, I reassumed the character I had relinquished barely a few days ago, aware that, this time, it would be mine for a long stretch, hopefully for life. A steely resolve took over. A sense of purpose solid enough to last. There was no room for childishness anymore, and there would be no more delusions about Ramzi and me. The life I wanted was within my control. It was time to grow up and be the man I aspired to be. A man like Ramzi. The fighter Baba called on me to become. A sadness washed over me. The promise that my confession would lead to absolution had collapsed as quickly as it had materialized. Losing Ramzi had not yielded, in the end, peace or closure. It had left me lonelier than ever.

Taking my silence as a sign of consent, Dr. Dajjani continued.

"Do you have sexual fantasies about men?"

"Yes, I do."

"Do you ever masturbate thinking about them?"

"Yes, I do."

"OK, Tareq, this is where you and I will have to start working together. I have a question for you."

"OK?"

"Do you believe in God?"

"Yes."

"And you go to church or the mosque to pray?"

"I go to church every Sunday."

"Wonderful."

"How did it go with Dr. Dajjani?" Mama asked after she picked me up.

"Fine," I answered. "I don't need to see her again. She agreed with

Baba. There is nothing to worry about." Mama's evident relief affirmed my decision; we would not speak of this again.

The rest was up to me.

◆ ◆ ◆

I stopped going to church. There was no longer a compulsion to ask for forgiveness; there were no more sins. I made sure there would not be. I cleansed my mind without any help; Dr. Dajjani and Christ were both redundant. I was in my final year in high school and buried in work. Even Tata could not argue with that. She tried, nonetheless.

"It would be good if you stepped away from your desk and took time to thank God for all that He has done for us. Pray, يا ابني, pray so that you would get the grades you want and into the universities you desire."

"Yes. I am praying, Tata, I am praying. I am thankful He is watching over me."

The lie did not feel like a lie on my tongue. There was no conscious decision not to pray. One day, there simply was the absence of prayer. I buried myself in work, studying late every night. "Studying is praying," Tata eventually relented, justifying my absence from church. Mama and Baba understood why I no longer had friends over. *We are all so busy. It is the final year of school.* And Ramzi? they asked. *He's overwhelmed at university.* Another alternate reality we all chose to embrace.

Like a recovering alcoholic, every day well lived was another day I had not slipped. Another affirmation of my strength, my ability to restrain myself, to become good. My mind had, overnight, become impervious to everything that had previously sullied it. The image of who I wanted to be was so tangible and clear and well defined, I embodied it fluently. I relished the intoxicating stillness that followed. No longer was I tormented by guilt or by the incessant questioning of what my fantasies meant. What kind of person they made me. Why I was the one who had provoked those darting shadows. Why I had fallen in love with Ramzi. Answers did not matter anymore, and neither did the questions. My mind tightened its grip around my thoughts with a determination that was as unforgiving as it was effective. Our own minds can enslave us in ways that would make our authoritarian leaders blanch.

Once the obsessive self-flagellation ended, I saw all that I should have been thinking about. Instead of existential demons, there were mediocre challenges, like college applications. *What do I want to study?* I had been robbed of time. On the cusp of that decision, there was no use trying to find the right answer. I copied Ramzi and chose engineering. "A pragmatic choice," Baba said. But my ambivalence toward my major came with a realization that was far more definitive: I no longer wanted to go to AUB. I applied to universities throughout the UK and US instead. "They have better engineering schools," I explained to my parents, who were perplexed by this unexpected change of tone. I had never mentioned any desire to be far from home, but overnight, that had become the only possibility I would entertain. "I earned this," I told them, negotiating with Baba as I had been trained to do, offering my academic record to advocate for my decision. When I got into school in London, I knew that my flight from Amman, from the region, had been set in motion.

To bewildered friends, I lied about the frost between Ramzi and me, gave some excuse or other. He must have done the same. Uncoordinated, we completed each other's fabrications, making sure to keep the letter unmentioned. The lengths we went to embellish signaled our desperation and, unusually in Amman, prevented further intrusions. There was a stink to our story that was too rotten even for their gossip. Or perhaps their gossip simply never reached me. In his wake was a blackness so complete that I failed to see his outstretched hand.

I did not return any of his calls. My newly acquired and very cumbersome mobile phone lit up every morning before I made it to school and throughout the day. For days, stretching into weeks, he texted me. Questions that were full of anticipation, yearning for an answer. *How are you? Are you OK? I'm worried. Why won't you call me back? Are we hanging out anytime soon? Can I come over?* I wanted nothing more than to answer—*Yes. Yes, come over, please*—to reclaim what was no longer there. But there was no way to undo what had been done. His messages taunted me with a fantasy that no longer existed. I looked at the dotted black envelope every time my screen came alive, and knew it was him before I opened it. I read his words and imagined the question marks at the end of each sentence floating away, untethered.

Accepting failure, his messages soon became monologues, updates on life. If we could not meander around our block, he seemed to say, he would tell me what he had to by text. He was adaptable. He would make do with this new medium until I was ready to see him again. *I went to the gym today. I miss my gym partner. I'm doing really well with the cigarettes—have cut down to half. Tanya called me last night.* Those words, too, hung limply in the space that had opened between us.

Then, one morning, his messages stopped. As I walked into the back door of the school, against the sound of honking cars, I realized my phone had not yet buzzed. I wondered if he was OK, if something had happened to him. I took my phone out and checked the screen. There was no envelope. I had good reception. The message could not have been lost. I put my phone back in my pocket and walked through the schoolyard.

His disappearance was so complete, it was as if he had only ever been a figment of my imagination. Where I lived, in the school courtyard, by the blue railings, around every corner in Amman—incredibly, he was in none of those places anymore. Wiped out from the space around me, he receded to the depths of my mind. An awareness of his absence pulsated within me, a sense of him everywhere I went. Until Christmas Eve, when I received the last physical reminder of his presence.

30

THE smell of turkey, bacon, and chestnuts wafted through the air and into the salon, where I went around with a box of matches, lighting candles that had their wicks covered in dust from the Christmas before. Flames reflected off the marble floor, shadows jumped around the walls of the dimly lit room, my family was getting ready upstairs, and I savored the lull before the festivities. Tata would be the first to arrive, returning from an earlier Christmas Eve Mass. There would be no need to ring the doorbell; the sound of Khalo berating her for walking too quickly up steps that were slippery with sleet and rain would alert me to their arrival. I would open the front door to find her dressed in the fur coat that only came out once a year. She would be doused in the perfume shared by all Palestinian Tatas, musky and fruity and inviting. She would hand me her Bible, the one with the golden letters sewn into its black leather, to read from later that night. My parents and brothers would come down. Cousins would arrive. Drinks would flow. Within minutes, the din of conversation would fill the space that had been carefully curated for the evening.

Every year, I got ready and came down before everyone else, seeking a moment of solitude with my favorite holiday. The ritual of lighting the candles had become meditative, allowing me to reflect on a year past and dream about the one peeking around the corner. Since turning twelve or thirteen, I had begun passing a commitment through those flames that I would, in the coming year, end my sinful existence. I would ask for forgiveness and express my appreciation for the Lord's patience over my constant failures, as if impatience might have manifested in a horrible intervention. I hoped our carols, the care with which we were celebrating the human birth of our God, the candles, might strengthen my prayers and carry them further than they might go when murmured from the side of my bed. Whispers born in flames, giving me resolve for the year ahead.

The Christmas after the letter was unlike past years. I went around lighting candles, but even with every wick coming to life, the setting around me remained dull. The lighting and the hymns and the smells wafting from the kitchen coalesced, as they did every year, but failed to turn to magic. Any sense that my ritual was placing me before God, before a divinity whom I wanted to serve and to whom I offered my vows, was gone. There was a void where a spiritual presence had previously been. Our Christmas traditions now appeared nothing more than a desperate attempt to cultivate the illusion of permanence. Nothing was permanent. The joy at having my family and friends under our roof was no longer a cause of celebration but a reminder of what would one day be lost.

I felt the parcel's presence before I saw it. A parcel that beckoned me to a time past, a time that promised warmth and comfort, although it had offered neither. There it was, nestled among the gifts Mama had wrapped under our tree, suggesting there was a normality that could be returned to. Implying that all that had happened between Ramzi and me was merely an unpleasant episode. It was his plea that in tradition there could be continuity, that rupture was not inevitable. If only I would return his calls, we could resume our togetherness. In placing it there, he was telling me that he was confident we would get past all that had transpired, and perhaps one day even joke about it. He did not yet see that we could never go back to any semblance of a shared life. There was no return. What had become known could not be made unknown, even if that *knowing* was lacking and devoid of anything other than shame.

How had he got it here? Mama must have let him in. She would not have thought much of it. We had been leaving gifts under each other's trees for years. Why would that year be any different? No one would have suspected that his absence in the weeks leading to Christmas was anything more serious than teenage turmoil. Certainly not anything as serious as him no longer being a part of our family. The unraveling of families, even adopted ones, is not done. We stick together. Mama was likely relieved a gift had materialized. *Had she invited him in for coffee? What did they chat about? Did he tell her how he was finding his new university life? Would she tell me if I asked?* I would not ask. Such questions did not fit with the person I was becoming.

I looked at the tree in the corner of the room, minimally decorated, hovering above an abundance of gifts. The pink made his easy to spot. I walked over and picked up the parcel. In the shadow of collapsed traditions, there was no reason to wait until everyone had arrived to unwrap presents. On that eve, opening his ode to tradition was a more fitting act than prayer. There was a white envelope taped onto the gift. A sharp pain sliced through me when I saw the *T* that he had scribbled on its front, like he had done on all his letters to me. I opened the note, the final one from the pile in the yellow box.

Dearest Tareq,

Well, it doesn't seem to me to be a white Christmas this year. I am sorry I didn't wrap it well and have no card but things went too fast the past two weeks and I swear I had no time to go shopping. Besides, I spent all my money already. I am now officially broke.

You've always liked this tie and I want you to have it. It will sure look nice on your new suit, the one you got for your aunt's wedding. I just couldn't buy anything for anyone else, and since you are really something, I thought I would give you something I own. I just stared at the tie and thought you deserved it.

I wish you a merry Christmas and a joyful holiday with your family, and of course, a happy new year later on. Will you get me a cigar this year, too?

I do wish you all the best in life in the coming years. I hope you lead a happy healthy life with your loved ones. Good luck to you my dear friend.

Truly yours,
R.

I was going to miss his neat handwriting, the way his lines never sloped or blended into each other. His was a steady hand. I knew which tie he had given me before I opened the box. I had told him I loved it often, pulling it out of his closet every time he was getting ready to go out and I happened to be in his room. Deep, dark black. Matte. A tie that should only be worn to a funeral or a black-tie event. I had been to neither. It exuded maturity. Only a certain kind of man could pull off its look, and I had both envied and adored the fact that he owned it.

I ran my fingers over its cloth as I had done several times before. It was thick and coarse, and I wondered if I would ever wear it. *Will you get me a cigar this year, too?* I pictured him sitting around his family, crestfallen at the realization that my gift had not appeared under his tree, despite what I imagined were his hopes in the days leading up to that eve. He must have known. His letter read like he was unsure whether he was going to be gifted a cigar, or be left wishing his friend a healthy life, one he feared he might no longer be a part of.

I put the tie around my neck and under the collar of my shirt, tying the knot a bit too closely, wanting the physical discomfort to distract me from the realization I had not yet confronted. *There is no going back to what had been.* I pulled the knot even tighter, feeling it crush my Adam's apple. I breathed to steady my nerves. I pulled in, just a bit tighter still, to stop the tears filling my eyes from spilling over. My throat caught. My heart ached. The veins in my temple pounded. For a fleeting few seconds, the first since the call, pangs tore at my chest as his parting gift dug into my neck.

III

31

EVERY generation in my family fled their homes. Every generation in Ramzi's did, too. Our grandparents, our parents; they fled war, death, gunfire. That is our fate, as Arabs, to flee. Is it not?

A picture stays with me. It haunted my dreams for nights on end after I saw it. The photo of Alan Kurdi's tiny body, washed onto land. His red T-shirt soaked as he lay facedown on a Turkish shore. His navy shorts, reaching below his knees, covered most of his legs. His little boots, which I imagined his father had lovingly put on to keep his feet dry on the rubber dinghy, made redundant. What caught my eye, and what I kept thinking about afterward, were his palms. Twisted upward even as his front pressed into the sand. His hands facing us even as his eyes are covered, like Naji al-Ali's Hanthalah. His final act to beseech the world, while crying into the cruel void of inaction.

There are more Lebanese citizens living outside Lebanon than on its lands: and this was before the country's criminal leaders presided over the third-largest non-nuclear explosion in the history of mankind, detonated smack in the middle of Beirut. The Assad regime's sprawling infrastructure of torture and death forced millions to flee from Syria. Libya, Yemen, Sudan—each has yielded its own refugees. Iraq, decimated by American and British imperialism, spewed forth its children into the ether. Our people today are throwing themselves into the Mediterranean. They are fleeing genocide, poverty, famine, dictatorship, or taking off in search of a better life.

Palestine to Lebanon, Lebanon to Jordan, from Jordan to where?

—

It is easy for me to claim flight as my rite of passage, a completion of our lineage, joining millions of others in making homes for themselves in strange lands. But Ramzi's eyes rest on me as I type these words, his admonishment burns into my back, calling on me to confront the hypocrisies, the lies we tell ourselves. He is, as always, correct. What right do I have to speak of flight? I have survived no wars. My scars are invisible, my movement privileged. More than two decades on and still I defer to him. I reconsider.

It is the journey of gradual estrangement, of alienation, that I am trying to convey. The feeling of not belonging that came to permeate my days. The conviction that one must remain hidden to live. Masked, covered. The inner bifurcation, the double consciousness. The exile of the authentic self. What I am thinking of is closer to the flight from reality that members of addiction groups invoke: the compulsion to exit one's truth by creating an alternative one. The succumbing to the allure of a new beginning that becomes irresistible, almost existential, with time, making escape inevitable. That is my individual flight, my walking away from that deathly disquiet that was sucking the life out of me. Not exile, then, but estrangement into a world that I hoped would provide a dignified life, one worth living.

32

THE night I left, East Amman stretched before me. I had driven up to the only spot in the city where I could be alone, a spot I had safeguarded from everyone, including Ramzi. One that was close to our old home in al-Abdali. From there, I could see the eastern half of the city. I had lost my connection to al-Abdali. Since childhood, we had moved steadily westward as we became better off. What had I left behind? My eyes lingered on the valley below me, my alienation from West Amman sparking a kinship with the eastern half, the unwanted one. The half we gazed upon, seated in our cafés and restaurants, but never really saw. *How well did we know our city, Ramzi and I?* It was far too late to be asking that question.

I sat on the hood of my car, the metal hot enough to scald my palms, and lit a cigarette. The heat of the summer day was just breaking, the sun's rays softening against the city's walls and rooftop water tanks. The muezzins from the minarets spread out before me crackled, as though an electric current ran through the valley and brought them to life. I shut my eyes, preparing to receive the cries of the imams, to let them wash over me as they called out to the faithful. Their melodic incantations lulled me then as they do today, even at the break of dawn, when their prayers nudge me out of sleep to remind me that I am home. In my teenage years, their chants filled my days with a comforting consistency. No matter how troubling things became, those imams were there meditating.

It was some time before it dawned on me that the اذان was nothing more than a poorly recorded tape that some disgruntled janitor had to play at a set time. Before my naivety broke, images of those imams filled my head: older men, kind, thoughtful, with groomed beards. Men who had just kissed their grandchildren goodnight and made their way over to their mosques. Men who sat cross-legged under the microphone, straightening their جلباب over their knees, closing their eyes, breathing into their bellies, reaching within their hearts to capture the ache that filled their chants.

الله أكبر.. الله أكبر، الله أكبر.. الله أكبر
أشهد أن لا إله إلا الله، أشهد أن لا إله إلا الله، أشهد أن محمدًا رسول الله، أشهد أن محمدًا رسول الله
حي على الصلاة، حي على الصلاة، حي على الفلاح، حي على الفلاح
الله أكبر، الله أكبر، لا إله إلا الله

Still, the recordings are resonant, the certainty embedded within their voices calms me. There is no room for ambiguity in their calls. *Prayer yields salvation. There is only the one God.* The hood of my car kept me warm against the evening chill, and I stayed put until the echo of the last verse had dissolved into Amman's dusk. An early flight awaited me, but I felt no urgency to leave. That night, my history felt as unknown to me as my Godless future.

Also unknown to me was that Amman and I were both bidding each other farewell. The finality of my departure to university was barely an intuition, a sense that after all that had happened, Amman might no longer tolerate my presence. There was no way of knowing, however, that our white city was also vanishing, soon to be consumed herself. Within the space of barely a few years, our small town would become a sprawling metropolis transformed by metal and concrete, as it offered homes to another mass of refugees who would frantically flee their own once-whole cities.

33

BY the time they made peace with my decision to go to London, Mama and Baba's doubt had given way to pride. "The top engineering school in the country," Baba beamed as he drove Mama and me to the airport in Amman. "London!" Mama kept repeating. "I love that city. All the parks. The ducks!" They started reminiscing about their time there, where they lived briefly after they fled Lebanon for Jordan. Following a hasty engagement in Amman to quiet the gossip, as her uncle had demanded, Mama and Baba had moved to London for a year, to explore different opportunities. In that city, their relationship morphed from a college romance into a marriage. Tata's diary records that day. *17 April 1977. Rima's wedding to Fadi. St Patrick's church in London. We couldn't attend and we were very upset about that.*

When I was ten, Mama and Tata took me and my brothers to visit for a week. They showed us all the sights as Mama retraced her steps in the city. The decrepit YMCA on London's Tottenham Court Road where she and Baba lived for months ("Tata thought it was filled with good Christian guests," Mama had chuckled), the office where Baba had gotten a gig as an administrator on the Strand, the redbrick St Patrick's Church in Soho Square where they had gotten married. Mama and Baba thought they might stay in London, but ultimately decided to return. "Better work," Baba said. "The sun, I needed the sun," Mama explained. To ease the heartache of leaving, they decided to go on a grand adventure for their honeymoon. They rented a red Alfa Romeo convertible and drove from London to Amman. "It took us a month!" Mama remembered. "One can never do that these days."

We landed at Heathrow days after my eighteenth birthday, armed with baggage that contained my yellow box filled with Ramzi's letters, warm clothes, toiletries, and enough supplies of "emergency medication" from Mama to open a pharmacy in my student accommodation. Baggage that contained, also, all of Amman's notions of *3eib* to guide me.

From the airport, I stepped into a city that was, in my imagination, firmly still my parents'. We had barely gotten into the cab at Heathrow when Mama turned to me. "You'll like this city. Sometimes I wonder why we left. We would have had British passports by now. But the sun!" As the taxi turned onto Evelyn Gardens, around the corner from my dorm, Mama grabbed my arm. "Ah, it's named after Tata! That must be a good omen." In my room, which was dark and poorly lit, I tucked the suitcase over the cupboard and looked around. Compared to homes in Amman, London has narrow staircases and coffin-like bathrooms that were just as bewildering to me as the double taps spewing either ice-cold or boiling-hot water. As I settled in my new city, vague memories resurfaced in unexpected spaces, as past shadows—mine, theirs—morphed into life.

◆ ◆ ◆

"My Arabian prince," Rishi—my neighbor down the hall who swiftly became my closest friend—mocked me one evening. "Toast for dinner again tonight?"

I was sitting in the communal kitchen, situated between his room and mine on the basement level, looking at the street above and the gray skies beyond. I had retreated here to escape the Bible study group that my roommate, John, was hosting in our room. "A Palestinian Christian," he had remarked when we first met during orientation. "Wow. I did not realize there were Christians in Palestine. You must join our services." I mumbled some excuse or other, defensively reminding him that Palestine is the birthplace of his religion, before swiftly extricating myself, not ready to reenter the ranks of the faithful. Instead, here I was, elbows leaning across the sticky kitchen table, munching on my toast, salivating over the smells of the curry Rishi was preparing as the windows steamed up.

"You mean you actually buy halal meat?" I asked, watching him stir the large pot of vegetables with lamb cubes.

He looked at me bewildered, as he did often in those early days, trying to make sense of this foreign creature learning to navigate London's mazes. I was evidently miles away from my homogeneously halal environment.

"Arabia, of course you do, man. How else can you eat halal meat?"

It had taken no time at all. I had become Arabia.

Over the months that followed, London slowly revealed herself. Our dorm, in the middle of Chelsea, was surrounded by mansions with manicured communal gardens, some of which had been appropriated by our university for student housing. Nestled in these lush neighborhoods, I observed my new home from the margins, absorbing the language, the disarming witticisms of the English, the mannerisms, ways of dressing, ways of being. I fell in love with the city despite itself. London's dampness drenched my clothes and stuck to my skin, leaving me perpetually cold. The food was underwhelming and underspiced; Ramzi would have hated it. He would have mocked the people, too: distant, guarded, timid. When not inebriated, they stuck to a regimented way of socializing that I struggled to master. *How had these people ruled the world?!* And the vast scale of the city forced a distance where closeness might have otherwise flourished, as it had in Amman.

Which is why I loved it. I was pulled into its urban energy, its speed. The city could take me anywhere and offer me anything. One more lost soul roaming around, suspended in time, with days so full, lifelessness could easily be overlooked. There were no darting shadows, barely even glimpses from passers-by. Gone was the sense of being observed. I walked down meandering roads or sat on the tube, sometimes even crossed my legs, and remained unseen. The emancipation was disconcerting, the autonomy overwhelming. One could do whatever one wanted without anyone ever knowing, let alone taking any interest. In my early months, I had no real compulsion to do anything; the mask I had fashioned in Amman had been firmly welded on. But the promise alone was titillating.

◆ ◆ ◆

The closest Metropolitan Police station was on Fulham Palace Road. "You need to register with the police," the passport control officer had said when I arrived in the UK on my student visa. His tone was stern and he spoke to me even though he was looking down at my passport. "You need to register within thirty days of arrival; otherwise, you will be in violation of your visa. Within thirty days, and after that, whenever there are any changes in your personal details—address, phone number, etc." He spoke slowly, to make sure I could follow these instructions, delivered in simple English, as if he were talking to a child. And this child was eager to please: I needed to locate the police station.

I walked from Evelyn Gardens to Fulham Palace Road, past mansions—"You know, Gwyneth Paltrow lives in one of these," Rishi, who had come along, told me—and up to a dull-looking redbrick building that was the station. I walked in, holding my passport open to the page of the visa, with pictures I had taken at the Snappy Snaps on the way.

"Why do you need to do this again?" Rishi asked.

"I have no idea, man. I was just told I need to do this every time I move flats or change my phone number."

"Even your number? Man, this is probably to keep tabs on you or some shit."

I shrugged and sat down on the row of plastic chairs lined up against the wall, opposite the police counters, a few seats away from a man who looked like he had been sleeping rough. The officer behind the counter, blond hair pulled into a ponytail, called on me. I smiled, handing over my paperwork, writing down my address and phone number on the form she slid toward me from behind her glass. She recorded all my details, and after a few minutes, produced a certificate, with my picture stapled on top and my address written in a box, stamped and signed. Eight other boxes lined the rest of the empty page. The exchange was smooth, effortless, and I looked at the certificate in my hand, oddly proud—at complying with the regulations, but also at this piece of paper, with my London address made official. *How will this page fill up? Where else will I live after Evelyn Gardens?*

34

NIKHIL entered my life a few weeks into term. He burst through the kitchen doors one evening, as Rishi and I were having dinner, a bundle of manic energy, pulling up jeans that were sliding halfway down his ass. He bounded across the table and introduced himself with a coy smile.

"Nikhil, from London," he said in a strong London accent. "Where are you two from?"

"Tareq, from Jordan," I said.

"Rishi, from Lancaster."

We rehearsed tired lines from freshman orientation week as Rishi and I exchanged glances. A lingering smell of weed emanated from Nikhil's clothes. His dark, almond-shaped eyes, with ridiculously long lashes, were glazed over. His small hand rested briefly in mine as he introduced himself without looking directly at me, his eyes turning sideways instead, nervous or bashful.

"Ya, I lived with my mum," he explained, "close by, but I moved into the room down the hall from you guys today. I missed orientation." He shrugged. "I was breaking up with my boyfriend."

"Sorry to hear that, man," Rishi said.

I nodded, drawn in.

From that first encounter, around the kitchen table, I wanted nothing more than to be in proximity to Nikhil, and I placed myself in his space—his messy room and his mother's home—more often than he might have appreciated. I was taken by everything mundane about him. How he woke up in the morning with bed hair and crumpled pajamas and made his way into the kitchen, hours after everyone else, for tea and toast. How he gave his mom a quick, self-conscious peck on the cheek whenever we swung by her flat to pick up his laundry.

How he talked to his mother about boys and university and drugs in one breath, without careful omissions or lies. How he parked his car, awkwardly and with little control. How he laughed out loud every now and then, for no apparent reason.

Everything that made him real, average, challenged what Amman had taught me about the impossibility of his life. I studied his nimble fingers as he rolled joint after joint, and saw his eyes lose their nervous energy every evening as weed filled his lungs. I was hungry to peer into his day-to-day, to feed a curiosity that had been held at bay my entire life. And he let me.

"You want one of these?" he asked every time he rolled a fat joint, with a twinkle in his eyes and a devilish grin. I held back, straitlaced, prudish. "Go on, Arabia, a joint won't kill you." Despite his fickle temperament with others in the dorm, he took a liking to me, lowering his guard to reveal playfulness, ribbing: "What's the matter, Arabia, the rain messes with your curls?" "Hurry up, Arabia, no chauffeur is going to pick us up." He let me into his smoky cave in the evenings, where we spent long hours watching each other, listening to Morcheeba and Portishead as London's skies drizzled outside.

One evening, I was sitting at the foot of his bed. He was stretched out, leaning back against the headrest, his feet, always cold, dressed in thick socks and tucked under my legs. The ashtray was on his stomach. He inhaled deeply from the joint and closed his eyes before blowing the smoke out.

"Ya, it's always been Mum and me," he was saying. "I never met my dad. My mum raised me in that flat, working as a nurse. Single mum, you know?"

I nodded, amazed. I had only ever heard of one divorce when I was growing up, and it had sent shock waves of gossip and mutterings throughout the city.

"You close to yours?" he continued.

"Yes, yes. I'm close to my dad. We're a tight family, we always have been. Although my brothers are closer to each other than I am to either of them." Mid-sentence, I realized that what I was about to say was that, while my brothers were close to each other, I was close to our neighbor, who had become like a brother to me. But then, that, too, was a distortion. Instead, I said, "I feel far from them now. I miss them."

"Sure you do," he joked.

"No, I do. I mean, yes, it's nice being here, getting some space from Amman. But it's also strange. I've never been this far or this alone."

"You're not alone, Arabia," he said, flexing his feet under my thigh.

I turned away, embarrassed. I pictured my body stretched out on the bed next to him, my head against his chest. Urges as comfortable and familiar as an old T-shirt. Dreams—of me getting into his sheets and holding his small frame tight as weed loosened him up, passing my hand over his taut belly, stroking its dark, curly hairs before reaching into the front of his pajama bottoms. I wondered what it would feel like to suck the smoke straight from his lips, to be the person he crawled back to after his nighttime escapades, to smell the scent of sleep on his pillows as he snored softly hours after I had woken. I squeezed his leg, just above his ankle. We fell into an easy silence as he took another drag. The rain drummed against the windowpane.

35

THE strobe lights brought her in and out of view. Blond, my height, green eyes, unfocused pupils. Another flash of light, my feet on the dance floor, wet, sticky, cigarette butts everywhere. The air smelled of stale beer. I was sweaty and tired, wanting to go home. Another strobe and I saw Rishi close by, flashing me a silly grin, winking. A sinking feeling. There was no turning back. I pulled her in closer and whispered that we should go somewhere quiet. She nodded and I turned to carve our way out through the bodies around us, pushing and cajoling, until we found a corner table in the lounge area. She sat on the leather sofa while I got us some gin and tonics. Three each to save us the bar waiting time. I sat down next to her, familiar with her body after an hour of grinding. She swung one leg across my lap and leaned in, her hair falling around my face, damp with sweat. She kissed me, her tongue cold from the ice of her drink. I tasted her lip gloss, and something else. Something sour. I wanted to pull back. Instead, I put my hands down on the leather of the sofa we were on and dug in.

"Are you sleeping with Erin now?" Nikhil asked me one night, his speech slurred.

We were sitting in his room, the sound of cars on the street above filling the space.

"Yes," I answered, flushed, aware next to him of what I could easily ignore elsewhere.

He looked at me, eyes full of disdain. I knew there was more to be said, that this was a betrayal, a tarnishing of what we had nurtured between us. But my words were still absent, my mask suffocating. I said nothing, hoping that he could see beyond what I projected, that he might continue to dwell with me in the margins. Understanding that this would be too much to expect. He smirked, shrugged his shoulders, the way he did when he was insecure, or ashamed, or nervous. The same way he had shrugged the day we met.

"You like it?"

"You know, sure," I mumbled. "She's hot."

He nodded, inhaling one more breath, and leaned across me to put the stub out in the ashtray. He did not offer me the usual puff I would have declined, and withdrew after that. I saw less and less of him as he spent more time at his mother's. That I missed him was inconsequential. After losing Ramzi, paying the highest price for letting my mask slip, it was no longer a mask; it was a second skin. I complained to Rishi about Nikhil's fickleness and carried on.

In club after club, dance party after rave night, Ramzi trailed me. His voice mingled with Rishi's and spurred me on. *Do what he would have done. Be the man he would have become in London. Prove to him that I am not the* khawal *he must now think I am.* Erin. Lucy. Li Mei. Nameless other lovers, picked up on the dance floor as club lights gave way to bedrooms. Kissing on street corners under sputtering rain. Waking up entangled in unfamiliar duvets. Lovers became friends and friends became lovers as I populated my newly created Facebook page, which I hoped he would see. A curated life—sterile, devoid of passion, picture perfect. In the wet city that got dark by the middle of the day, Amman stayed within me, Ramzi beside me.

◆ ◆ ◆

Rishi and I are standing outside Knightsbridge station, right next to Harrods. The pavement is filled with people. Opposite the street, there are cafés offering argileh and tables so packed that a cloud of smoke hovers above the clientele. Luxury cars are parked outside: Lamborghinis and Ferraris and Aston Martins. Rishi nudges me.

"You recognize any of these guys sitting here?" he chuckles.

"Nah, man. I don't know any of these folks."

"Sure you don't. My Arabian prince. Why don't you get us one of these?" he asked, nodding toward the cars.

"My brothers would kill for one," I laughed.

A man walked by, a tourist, speaking to his partner, a woman in a hijab, in Arabic. He stood by us, put his shopping bags down, and fumbled in one of them, looking for something. He pulled out a cigarette pack and lit one. He then turned to her, sweeping his arm in front of him, as if inviting her to take in the magnificent view.

"Look, look," he said to her. "Just look at this pavement. It's sparkling clean, I could lick it. Not a single piece of rubbish."

She nodded, bored. I tuned in, anticipating the lecture to follow.

"This is how they do it. They're civilized people. The clean streets! The progress! They take care of their cities. They keep things in order. If this was back home, this place would be filthy, rubbish everywhere. والله احنا بجم. We don't deserve our cities."

She nodded again as Rishi nudged me, aware that I was listening in on their conversation, curious as to what was being said.

"It's nothing, man," I explained. "The man is just hating on the Middle East. Let's go."

I had not quite admitted it yet, but I, too, was hating on the Middle East. Even as I performed for Ramzi in London, imagined his eyes trailing me, my alienation from the region grew. This had, in truth, begun linguistically in the days when Ramzi and I were still Ramzi and me. Arabic carried within its folds all that society harbored against me. It was the language of my bullies, of Mustapha Aboud, and I had kept hitting its walls and feeling alien in its spaces. Vileness had been injected into any articulation of self I could have identified with. It made me feel dirty—weak, emasculated. I could not find myself in its words and was unable to grow in its sounds. *How could I live within a language that portrayed all my desires as repugnant? Who would I have become amidst all that disfiguration?*

Without any thought, I had always written to Ramzi in English, and with every letter, the distance between myself and Amman had expanded, affirming something he said to me, over and over again, as if it were a compliment. *You do not belong here*, he repeated. In the contempt he harbored for Amman, goodness belonged elsewhere—here, only the rotten stayed and festered. I grabbed on to his thoughtless banishment, wearing it like a badge of honor, not understanding that what he was really saying was that I was not welcome. *It would be best if you stopped coming over.* I internalized his indictment and allowed English to colonize my thoughts. Embraced it as a better language, the language of power and sophistication.

In London, with every passing day, I became more confident speaking in this foreign tongue, and without much thought, I relinquished my Arabic. I became punctual, more punctual than the English. I rarely ate Arabic food and played, exclusively, Western music. I read voraciously, all the Western literature I picked up in secondhand bookstores on Charing Cross Road. Embraced alien concepts, like atheism, to retroactively explain my alienation from Jesus Christ, and held on to them with a zeal that was frightening, more concerned with finding alternative identities than searching for the one that fit best.

And without realizing when I tipped over, I found that I had grown disdainful of being "Arabia." I was nothing like those men loitering around luxury stores in London, even less like the others spending their days in argileh cafés or hanging around Edgware Road. I wasn't like those men I left behind in Amman, either. I was enlightened, not closed-minded: an Arab who was liberal the way the English were liberal. I was an Arab who was closer to the colonial power than to those sorry souls who had been colonized. A subject who had now settled in the heart of the metropole. *A cosmopolitan. A citizen of this world. Diversity! Tolerance! I now have gay friends!*

It took no time at all to let go of the identity that had forsaken me. Instead, I performed being Arabia in jest, embracing images that would make Edward Said cringe. After Arab men crashed into the Twin Towers, I was vindicated. "See," I said to anyone who might listen, "there are many crazies back where I come from. Saudi Arabia is in the Stone Age. What do they expect would happen if they run the country the way they do? They create men who murder others for religion. How ignorant. How anarchic. No, no, Rishi. I am not Arabia. I am not like them."

36

I CALM my nerves. *My visits are short. There is no reason to be anxious. I am only going for a few days*, I think to myself, as the queue at Heathrow pulls me out of London's ecosystem toward Amman's, out of anonymity toward familiarity. I stand apart from fellow passengers, many of whom I suspect are Jordanian. I fashion myself a foreigner, a Londoner, and look around with thinly disguised contempt. My spine is straighter than it used to be. Where there was once timidity, arrogance now prevails, protecting me from the darting shadows. I roll my shoulders as I wait to board.

In Amman, my first few minutes back home are surreal. Baba and Mama look the same, but are altered somehow. I bend over to give Tata a hug. She has aged—and only in her face, her frailty, do I see the passage of time, do I understand that, in stepping back into my home, I have been outside of it, separate from it. In minutes rather than days, that distance is crossed, as I am pulled back into Amman's daily rhythms. But the feeling stays with me, confirming that I am no longer wholly of this place. Another life exists, an alternative one, and in that sense, I am not consumed by Amman, by its claustrophobia. I come to it, rather, with a sort of hedged presence, arriving back on the condition that I will soon be leaving.

During that trip, I visit a drab and dirty government building to renew some paperwork. Cars are parked haphazardly outside, and the office is surrounded by small kiosks set up by entrepreneurial men offering to fill out forms and complete paperwork in exchange for some coins. Their entire business relies on the labyrinthine process of completing any task in governmental offices, on having unlocked the secret to the chaos. I decide to take this task on myself. I go in and out of rooms, up and down staircases, join queues and ask around in offices that need scrubbing and better lighting, serviced by muddy bathrooms that reek of piss and shit.

I take my place in a queue I guess is mine. Men in gray suits and dusty black shoes and women wearing exasperated faces jostle around me, thrusting their paperwork in the officer's face.

"Excuse me," I say softly to no one in particular, "there's a line. Wait your turn."

A woman in a hijab on my right mutters at how rude and uncivilized we are all being. I nod. *An ally*, I think, but then see her elbow the man next to her, hoping to embarrass him into making room for her. It works. The man bows to allow her to pass, then reaches over her head to put his paperwork in front of the officer. I stand my ground, anger swelling, as elbows and stares shove me to the side.

"Excuse me," I say, more aggressively this time, "there's a line."

And then the *tut*. English passive-aggressiveness amidst the least passive crowd there ever was. I tut and push forward, hesitant, hoping not to offend anyone, wanting nothing more than to save my place in the queue. *That is my right*. More pushing and growling.

"There's a line!"

Anger gnaws at my insides as men and women look at me in bewilderment. *Tut tut tut*. They are having none of it, and it is clear what they think of me as I desperately tut and cluck my way through the crowd. Superiority keeps my feet glued to the ground as the people try to nudge me out of the way. A couple of hours and tens of customers overtake me before my determination is worn out. Begrudgingly, I begin forcing myself to the front, elbowing people around me. *They are all rude anyway*, I tell myself. I get to the front and hug the counter, putting my papers right in front of the officer's face.

No reaction. The officer's work is neither speedy nor lazy, divorced from the mania around us. He carries on, barely lifting his eyes, even though my papers are almost touching his forehead. Once he finishes the document in front of him, he reaches up and grabs the closest folder threatening to poke his eye out: my own. He looks at my application, then up at me, and asks some questions. I answer, self-consciously, in my tired Arabic. Bemused looks all around. This is my nightmare.

"انت اجنبي؟" the man behind the counter asks, with a real or imagined hint of sarcasm in his voice.

"No, no, I'm not foreign. I was born and raised here."

A nod. I know the thoughts rushing through his mind. *Those damned privileged kids, they travel to foreign countries and come back here thinking they're better than us.* Or, *Poor little Baba's boy is upset he had to come and deal with this paperwork on his own in this shithole.* Or, worst of all, *What a sissy: He speaks like a girl. His cheeks even flushed when I spoke to him.* I am desperate to leave, and as soon as he hands me back my paperwork, I mumble a thank-you and walk out of the building into the blinding sunlight and the heat, more certain than ever that I cannot live in Amman.

A single continuum connects that civil servant to every darting shadow, and every darting shadow to the country's trajectory, its history and future. *That queue, the officer's withering look, these are the reasons we will never amount to anything,* I think as I leave that government building. Ramzi's loathing of this place has, somehow, become embedded within me—it is a loathing embedded within many of us—an endless malaise. I, too, want nothing to do with Amman anymore. There is something rotten at the core.

37

"WHAT do you think of Chemical Ali?" Andrew asked me one morning as we milled outside the hall for our lecture on system controls and dynamics.

"Who?" I asked, wondering how I had missed this nickname for Ali, the Bahraini guy in our class.

"You know, Saddam Hussein's minister."

"Oh. Not much," I shot back, abruptly ending the conversation, hoping the coolness of my voice would deflect from my embarrassment.

Ali Hassan al-Majid was not yet a familiar name to me, despite his infamy. In the homes we grew up in, Ramzi and I, heroic wartime tales from parents and grandparents were divorced from politics. Their messiness was scrubbed out, left in the distant past, so that they would not threaten the peace of our present in Amman. Uproarious banter collapsed into whispers when my parents had friends over and the chat turned to politics. The sudden lowering of their voices would wake me up at night, and I would strain to hear snippets, words exchanged in hushed breaths. "The walls have ears," Mama used to say, as I envisioned human ears tucked away in the corners around our home. Our parents' lives had come unhinged too many times, and—rightly or wrongly—they decided it was enough for us to have been given shelter, after Haifa and Beirut. To demand more was a betrayal of that gift. There was an unacknowledged pact with our host country: To live, we had to be silent.

I had landed in London well trained to hold on to that silence, to suppress thought, to focus on the mundane. The Second Intifada was raging in the background, peppering conversations here and there, appearing in headlines on the evening news throughout my university years. I felt vaguely implicated and entertained inane conversations with friends. But this was nothing more than passing commentary. I shifted my gaze from the region, immersing myself instead in the study of thermodynamics, fluid mechanics, mathematics. I mapped fluid movement in pipes, wrote out eloquent integration sequences, grounded myself by designing intricate power plants. In those schematics, there were only right answers and wrong ones. An outcome either worked or it had to be revised. If one followed the steps to differentiate equations, correct answers could be had. Mistakes could be fixed, steps retraced. It was a refuge, a way for me to control my mind, to make it impenetrable, as Baba had counseled me I must.

◆ ◆ ◆

The bench I am sitting on is soaked from the night's rain. Cold water seeps through my jeans. Mid-March. *Amman is well into spring by now.* I grumpily pull my coat closer and exhale into my scarf, fogging up my glasses. I am too cold to unwrap myself and get up, so I sit clutching at whatever body heat I can trap. Memories flood my mind. Our family holiday to London, years ago. Mama, my brothers, and I standing right by this bench, where I had ended up before realizing that this spot was familiar.

Hyde Park was glorious that day. My brothers and I were feeding the swans in the round pond, none of us having seen any before. Nadim was obsessed, and even though Mama had warned us not to step too close to the edge, he wanted to pet a swan that was hovering around waiting for crumbs. Mama was distracted talking to Laith for a second when Nadim leaned over. Before we knew it, the swan was towering over him, manically flapping its wings and sending water and feathers flying in the air. Nadim slipped into the pond as Mama rushed over. Then his wailing. We were all laughing hysterically as Mama picked him out of the water and held him at a distance to protect her clothes from the dripping grime. She tried to comfort him as waves of laughter racked her body. I had never seen her laugh like that, laugh so hard that tears ran down her face.

The war drums have been beating louder. A month ago, there had been a million-person march against the Iraq War. I had been swept up by the wave washing over campus, pulled into its energy. The blinders I had grown accustomed to in Amman were becoming more cumbersome in London. Questions were being formed where before there had been none. I had arrived at the scene ambivalent, feeling tenuously responsible for representing Iraq, but wholly incapable of articulating anything beyond basic opposition to war. Exiting Green Park station, I began marching in lockstep toward Piccadilly Circus, unsure, curious. I had never seen anything like this before: the vocal, unabashed calling out of a prime minister, of a government. The chanting—rhythmic, impassioned—resonated with me even as I feared possible repercussions. *Would my presence here make it onto my record, on the Police Certificate?* I had not yet broken out of my own insignificance.

But the swell of the crowd seeped through my armor. The tyranny with which I policed my voice and gestures, reinforced year after year at school, the self-consciousness with which I had learned to walk and tighten my wrists, the mask I so desperately guarded, dissolved in the mass of people. I began chanting, softly at first, then louder and louder. I raised my fist, my heart pounding, feeling energized by the protesters next to me. Feet against pavement, my body took over, confidently, assuredly, as my mind surrendered. All the unanswered and unasked questions gave way to an embodied rush, like Ramzi's fistfights or Mama's impassioned speech in the protest Baba recounted to us when we were younger. All merged into that fleeting moment as I walked, utterly consumed, untamed. *No War in Iraq, No War in Iraq.*

On the bench a month later, the image of me crisscrossing tape across the windows of my bedroom in al-Abdali in 1991 swims into my mind. I was in my tae kwon do class when the three distinct blasts of Mama's horn burst through the auditorium. I scrambled out and into the car, quiet for the drive back, the tension in Mama's body palpable. At home, dressed in my white uniform, with the brown belt tied around my waist, we began preparations. Mama and Tata brought out the tape, the wide, brown kind that is used for packing, and instructed us to cover the periphery of each window in our house, before completing an X in the middle. As Laith and I worked the windows, Mama and Tata stacked canned foods in one of the rooms in the back and told us to pile our favorite books and toys there when we were done. I asked Mama if we could bring my tortoises in from the garden, and she assured me they had their own basements outside.

For days leading up to the Gulf War, she and Tata had been busy sewing masks. Baba came back one evening with blue cotton masks, the ones surgeons use in operating rooms. Mama and Tata layered those with socks and asked us to put them around our mouths and noses. I woke up one night to hear Mama and Baba arguing down the hall in their bedroom.

"Why couldn't you get the real masks? You must know someone at the office who knows someone. These cotton ones will not work." She was frustrated.

I could not make out his answer, but remember thinking that the masks did work. Laith pretended to be a zombie when Mama tied the mask around his face. I screamed as he chased me around the house.

I pass my fingers over the calling card I've bought on the way to Hyde Park. I know what has to be done. "Are you OK?" Mama immediately asks when she picks up the phone. "Why are you calling? It's not Sunday yet. What's happening? You sound down." I reassure her. "There is nothing urgent, everything is fine, except I need a break from London. I want to come home. People are saying the war is around the corner and I want to be with you all."

"No way. Listen to me. There is absolutely no reason for you to come back. Stay in London—it's safer there."

"بس ماما . . ."

"Why would you come back? Nothing will happen here. This has nothing to do with us. Don't miss classes!"

"Mama, I cannot think of being in London if something happens there. What if I can't get to you or get you on the phone? I will lose my mind. I want to be home."

"Stop being dramatic. Nothing is going to happen in Amman."

The next day, March 19, 2003, unbeknownst to my family, I board a Royal Jordanian flight to Amman. This time, the queue at the check-in counter has no familiar faces—evoking trepidation, not relief. I am one of a handful of Jordanians boarding a plane full of foreign journalists and aid workers making their way through Amman to Baghdad. Halfway over Europe, our pilot informs us that our flight will be the last to land. From then on, civilian flights are to be grounded indefinitely to make room for American and British fighter jets heading to Iraq. I feel sick. The person next to me, a white British man, turns over toward me.

"Lucky for us we got on this flight," he says.

"Ya, exactly. I wonder when they'll start bombing," I reply, mouthing the unbelievable.

"Probably after midnight, shortly before dawn. Don't think that will give me enough time to get to Baghdad before it starts."

"You're going to Baghdad tonight?"

"Yes. I'm a journalist. I was told you can get a taxi from the airport. Do you know if that's right? I have all my luggage with me. Gas masks. First aid kit. Camera. I'm all set."

"I have no idea," I answer, visualizing Mama's sad sock masks and thinking my luggage, replete with books and snacks, equally inadequate. "I've never been."

"Is that not where you're heading?"

"No. No. My family lives in Amman."

My transit home had become part of a commuter route to a war zone. Thinking of the bombs that would soon rain on Baghdad, a city that had only existed in my mind as one of the revered centers of Arab intellectual and cultural life, a thought crystallized. One that would change the course of my life—not immediately, but like all moments of critical truth, slowly, assuredly, and consistently over many years. Sitting there, chatting to the well-meaning British man, I realized I was, in fact, and despite all performances to the contrary, an Arab man who was scared and filled with foreboding, with a force I had not realized was within me. I was consumed by a ravaging sadness that carried the weight of ancestral pains and injustices. An anger, also, at the arrogance of those fighter jets that would, soon after we landed, whizz overhead.

I leaned back, closed my eyes, and thought of the millions of families, like mine, that were scrambling to put pathetic sock masks on their faces, and I began praying to a God I hadn't spoken to in years, appealing to him to have mercy on Iraqis that night.

38

OPERATION Iraqi Freedom. 5:34 a.m. March 20, 2003. It began four hours after my flight landed in Amman. Iraqi freedom delivered on the backs of American and British killing machines. Another continuum: from the eyes of the passport control officer who first greeted me at Heathrow, informing me of my duty to report to the police station, up to the British and American fighter jets swooping in over Baghdad. Our cities were being scapegoated, again, as playgrounds for murderous Americans and Brits. This time, as images of Iraqis handing out flowers and chocolates to American tanks driving through Baghdad blasted into our living room, my family talked and argued.

"They think we're stupid," Mama kept saying, shaking her head. "They just remembered they want to free the Iraqi people after starving them for a decade."

A Mama we had only heard of before, envisioned as a heroine in Baba's memories, flickered before our eyes. We marveled at America's military might, which took one of the most feared dictators in the region and broke him like an elephant might a twig. There was no euphoria in our house. No illusion, not for a pitiful second, that America's occupation was any less deadly or vile than Saddam's dictatorship. We grieved the destruction of a grand Arab metropolis, one reduced to a notch in the bedpost of war criminals. Voices around the screen shook with emotion as Mama, Baba, and Tata relived past traumas inflicted by different incarnations of those same perpetrators. We had seen what occupation looks like. There we sat, three generations of Palestinians, painfully familiar with its reality.

The rage Mama carried finally felt fitting, just as Baba's pragmatism was comforting.

"Baba, the Americans are not idiots. They know what they're doing," he kept telling my brothers and me, intermittently taking puffs on his cigar. "This is not a joke for them. They have a plan for the Middle East."

The search for a rationale for our murder made sense. Otherwise, we would have had to face the truth that—for them—our lives were totally expendable.

Our white city, as Mama had predicted, was left unscathed—at least in the beginning. With time, it would become yet another facet of Iraq's devastation as refugees settled in, waiting for an interminable war to end. Even as the city remained physically whole, we knew how fleeting stability was—*our cities will be devastated once more*—and how incomplete, given the tragedy of our Iraqi neighbors. Scars etched on those fleeing war and those hosting them.

After a summer in Amman, I return to London. I stand next to Rishi on Battersea Bridge, where we stop on our daily walk back from university to look at the bright moon shining down on the Thames. It is dark, even though the day is barely past its midpoint. He asks about Amman, about the war. I grasp for words.

"Something is different about you," Rishi, perceptive, brilliant, says. "I can almost feel you withholding things that are on the tip of your tongue."

I nod, without denying this time.

"There are things to be said. I just need to learn how to say them."

I sit on my bed, in my room, and look back. The assault on Iraq is fresh, poking, unsettling me. Something has been dislodged. I am brimming with more questions than answers. Where I had been surefooted in the darkness, I am now clumsy and uncertain. My engineering classes and the people around me are suddenly distractions, blinders I want taken off. Amman, in the wake of that violence, beckons me to return. The anger around me that summer has given way to a solidarity, a pride, I have never allowed myself to see or touch. As Baghdad fell into American hands, an allegiance murmured within me.

IV

39

DARK rooms gave me freedom. Unseen was how I thrived. The only way to face unanswered questions was by fleeing. The self I had fabricated in London was not the answer; the Iraq war had shown me that. The city had become familiar, assuming elements of home, and what I needed was to be in strange lands, where I could disappear. Lands I would not sully with my perversions. From the university's exchange programs, I sought the furthest destination I could run to, and, as the plane ascended over a wet London, I promised myself that in the parallel universe where I was to spend my third university year, a reckoning awaited. With all the efficiency of an engineer, I would bend time and space by coming to Sydney, pause life, and extricate myself from its relentless grind until I could make sense of it.

I first noticed Sam walking into the grand dining hall of our college, on the edge of campus. With a head full of brown curls and a hearty laugh, Sam was in everyone's way, talking to this girl and that boy, smacking this one's ass and that one's shoulders. He was the center of everyone's attention. I turned around and carried on, expecting our paths never to cross. But Sam's room—where he dimmed the lights, put on Café del Mar–type chilled tunes, and spread an array of drugs on the coffee table—became the hangout in our dorms. Barely a few days after arriving in Sydney, I found myself standing in his doorway. He glanced at me and, without skipping a beat in the story he was animating to a group of enthralled listeners, summoned me in. I got myself a beer and settled by the arm of the ratty blue couch next to his bed, taking in the vibe.

Against the chaos of the party, our eyes locked, again and again. Wordless though our exchange was, the warmth on my skin where his glances fell told me everything I needed to know. After some time, he made his way over, smiling with a confidence that acknowledged whatever it was that had passed between us. His eyes were unusually brown, almost orange, and I wondered if he was wearing colored contacts. His face was more potholed with pimples than I had realized at a distance. His teeth were crooked beneath his full lips, and his curly hair was frayed around his ponytail. He offered me his hand, his skin smooth, his palm fleshy, wet. I pulled away too quickly, and worried that I may have offended him. He did not seem to notice and settled in the space next to me on the couch, a bit too close.

"Someone had to make the first move," he grinned.

"Yup. But this couch is so comfy it was never going to be me."

"You're going to regret you said that in a second."

"Why?"

"I picked this couch up from the corner of the street outside. Someone had thrown it out and it was wet and dirty and looked like it had bedbugs."

"What the fuck? Are you serious?" I jumped off.

He chuckled.

"Relax. I am serious, actually. But I got it cleaned properly. Don't worry. Nothing is going to bite your ass tonight."

I sat back down, just as close as I had been. Question after question he asked, about my name, where I was from, what had brought me to Sydney. My answers were unsophisticated. The practiced responses offered time and again, to the usual string of inquiries, were flimsy when presented to him. I wanted to hold his gaze, to prove to him and to myself that I could keep him engaged. To feed, also, my own curiosity about him. He was Syrian, born in Australia and raised all over the world as his family moved every few years for his father's job. His parents were born and raised in Damascus. He grew up in a very Arab home, he said, before pointing to the weed spread out on the table.

"My parents would not be happy," he smirked.

He talked about visiting Amman and Beirut while recounting memories from school in Amsterdam and home in Melbourne. He dropped hints about this or that girl as he rested his hand against my thigh. Gone were the typical markers that might define him. In the palm of his hand, home and exile merged; he was at once of my world and entirely foreign to it. I was completely absorbed, oblivious to the people around me, who were beginning to thin out. *He is without structure*, I thought. A man who was entirely fluid, existing between boundaries, flitting between straightness and queerness, foreignness and indigeneity, seriousness and lightheartedness, without acknowledging, or caring, how unsettling such transitions might be. He scorned the boundaries that had dictated the course of my life and that had made any sense of happiness or peace unattainable. Our bodies were almost touching, and I could smell the beer and weed on his breath. I wanted to be closer, to confirm his physicality, to show myself that there was, despite all this fluidity, solid matter anchoring him. He laughed and looked at me mockingly.

"What?" I said, feigning annoyance.

"You looked like you were gone somewhere serious. I lost you for a second."

"Oh, sorry."

"Nah, man. Don't apologize. What were you thinking about?"

"I'm not sure."

"These fuckers are weird, aren't they?" he said, pointing to the people in the room.

"Ya. They're very white."

He laughed.

"What? You don't think you're white? You're paler than me and you have green eyes."

I squirmed.

"I'm just pulling your leg, T-man, relax." He laughed again, squeezing my knee. "Jeez. You are one serious dude, aren't you? Here, you need one of these," he said, as he leaned forward and began breaking up leaves to roll a joint.

I watched him mix the weed with tobacco and pile it onto a long paper. He placed the filter at the end and rolled it swiftly. He lit up and took a deep breath.

"Man, I don't know what I would do without this shit. What would our 'rents think if they saw us here?" he added, handing me the joint.

This time, I took it. The tip was wet with saliva, but I inhaled anyway.

"Lucky for me, mine are on the other side of the globe," I said, choking on the smoke.

"I hear you. Must be tough, though, being here on your own. Don't worry. You'll come to Melbourne and meet mine. You'll have your Aussie Arab family up in your business soon enough."

I was mesmerized—repulsed and attracted in equal measure. My toes and fingers started going numb and my mind became lucid. Although stoned, I recall exactly my thoughts that night—or rather, the memories of my thoughts. Sam's demeanor made me aware of my rigidity, of the control I imposed on my life, of the weight of my determination to live by Amman's expectations. I had learned to compartmentalize my yearning for Nikhil, to contract my muscles to move and act a certain way, to not breathe the political truths saturating the very air around me. I had thoroughly hidden myself from myself. And now, conflicting feelings gave way to clarity. Here was this soul whose entire being catered solely, unapologetically, to his own impulses. Someone who embraced shapelessness as the only structure one needed.

We spoke all night, and as people left his room, the universe shrank to the space between our bodies, nestled on one end of the couch, where he stayed even after friends left his side. The steel scaffolding that I had painstakingly assembled to hold me up, like the blueprints of my engineering design sheets, slid, molten and fluid, down my body. Hot metal that ran across my chest and my back and between my thighs. I was amorphous, undefinable, oozing out of the contours of my skin.

A few days later, he passed a note under my door. *Meet me in front of the dorm at 9 p.m. Bring a sweater. Sam.* At six that evening, I saw him at the dining hall, dressed as we all were in formal clothes and gowns, waiting to be served in this space that was trying hard to emulate the British Oxbridge tradition. I looked across the table at him and raised my eyebrows. *You'll see*, he mouthed, giggling at my confusion. After dinner, I tried to read, but was impatient, waiting for minutes to pass. Shortly before we were meant to meet, I made my way down.

"Where are we going?" I asked. "Tell me."

"Relax, man, you'll see. Just chill."

He had a full backpack. We walked out of the dorm and down the road, running to catch the bus into town.

"Just tell me," I nagged like a petulant child.

"Relax, you don't want to ruin the surprise, do you? It's just something I want to show you. Just wait," he said, which hardly eased my curiosity.

We got off near the circular quay, down by the harbor, and I looked out into the water. I had only been in Sydney a short time, and the bridge, lit up at night, had not yet lost its power to bring me to a halt. Facing the water, we turned right, the bridge behind us, and walked toward the gardens of the opera house, dazed in white light, looking otherworldly. There were some people ambling about, but the space was mostly deserted. We headed toward the steps of the opera house as I tried to make sense of his plans. *Had he gotten tickets for the opera?* I wondered, before quickly dismissing the thought. Although I barely knew him, I had a sense that such a gesture would be unlike him, and the tickets were too expensive anyway. Instead, by the steps, he veered right, away from the opera house and toward the botanical gardens that stretched behind it.

"We can't go there," I said. "The gardens are closed."

He chuckled.

"Yes, I know they're closed."

"So, why are we still walking in this direction?"

"Just trust me."

I followed, nervous, as always, fearful of breaking rules, of getting caught. He reached the walls stretching around the garden and swung himself up. I stayed put.

"Come on, let's go. Quick."

"Sam, I'm not sure about this."

"Just get up, T-man. Stop nagging and get up."

I shook my head and swung myself up, holding on to the fence for balance. We walked along the edge for a few meters and around the corner, where somehow, a small space appeared between the fence of the gardens and the drop down to the water below. We were standing on what looked like a cliff wall, on the outer side of the fence. With the sea below us, and the fence behind us, we climbed up the rocks for a couple of meters until we arrived at a small plateau that resembled a cave entrance. But there was no cave, just a slight dip, a cavity in the side of the cliff, like a naturally designed rock bed. He paused there and looked out into the water before turning to me with a huge smile across his face, as proud as a toddler after their first step. The sails of the opera house towered to our left, the water sang beneath our feet, the lights of Mattawunga Bay shone on the far side of the harbor, and we were alone, just the two of us, in this enchanted place.

"Now you're quiet?" he joked.

"How? How did you find this?"

"Don't worry, T-man. You'll learn to trust me and stop asking questions with time. Come, help me put this out."

He pulled a blanket out of his backpack and spread it over the jagged rocks. We sat down and I stretched my legs. I looked out toward the water. The air was salty and damp, unlike Amman's. *This*, I thought to myself, *this is my cocoon here in Sydney.* I turned back to Sam, who looked nothing like Ramzi, and who was making a lot of noise rummaging through his backpack. He pulled out his weed kit, some beers, and a pack of chips.

"For the munchies!" he laughed.

40

AFTER every sunset, I pushed against Sam's door. We would settle between the bed, coffee table, and couch for the night. The weed kit would be spread out on the table, clinical, primed to transport us to our nocturnal selves. Amman, with all its proscriptions, felt like the faraway planet it was—no longer able to tighten its grip around my throat.

Night after night, our journey unfolded as a single conversation, interrupted only by the mundane necessities of life: studying, sleeping, eating. For months, we smoked and talked until the early hours, when the rays of light dispelled the smoky remnants of our emotional voyages. The red slashes of the sky, peeking in through his window, reminded me of the dawn athaan and evoked their own spirituality at the beginning of each day. Others stopped coming to his room; it was only us. With Sam, as with lovers to come, we existed in a suspended state of utopia. One that is by default fleeting, disconnected, and exclusive, sheltering us from our lives only for as long as we sustained its sanctity.

Sam had a need to understand his impulses, those truths he carried within him as an Arab man without quite understanding where they had come from, and he latched on to everything I had to offer. I came to him with Amman's burdens of religion and masculinity and chauvinism and war. I laid those at his feet, exhausted by having borne their weight since I was a child chipping paint on the blue railings, delaying my descent into the courtyard. With him, I could articulate unspoken thoughts, expunge them from my body and hold them in the space between us, so that they were no longer solely mine, but ours to grapple with. Just as I had emptied my bag of darting shadows every night before going to bed, presenting its contents to Christ, so I brought out everything for Sam, my chosen witness. I told him of Tata's crucifix, of kneeling by the side of my bed. I spoke of my comfort every time I crossed my hand over my face and chest.

"Until I began hating religion," I said. "Its institutionalized rituals."

I had heard someone in London say those words, and thought they sounded intelligent. What I really wanted to say was that I hated my God for failing to absolve me. Whichever way I said it, Sam understood. My censors drugged, I spoke of bullying, and he defanged a million past insults. I told him of shame, and *3eib*, and honor, and in his wondrous capacity to reshape things, he turned them around. No longer were they sources of guilt or judgment, but signs of community, of love and protection, tradition and meaning. He broke words and expanded their reach to make room for me. He would challenge, ask, want to learn more. In return for my insight, he gave me freedom.

One evening, I told him to come over to my room instead of meeting at his and sank into the cushions I had arranged on my balcony, enjoying the breeze blowing in from the harbor. The branches of the tree outside my dorm room swayed toward me, reminding me of Baba sitting out in the evening air in Amman. I lit a cigarette and opened a book I had been reading about the indigenous peoples of Australia, but I was having trouble concentrating. I knew why I had invited Sam to my room. I lit another cigarette as he walked in and hopped onto the balcony, landing on the cushions next to me, grinning. *Our session is in order*, he seemed to be saying.

It was inevitable that we would speak about Ramzi. This person who had become the most intimate companion to my thoughts, like a child's invisible friend. *How would I introduce him? What was my story?* A sadness had anchored itself permanently in my body after I hung up the receiver, that moment which had upended my life and left me seeking cover. After four years, I had no idea where the real Ramzi was, or if indeed there was a real Ramzi. *Had he always been a figment of my imagination?* I was finally peering out, ready to have the conversation that, in another world, I may have had with him.

"Sam, I need to tell you something."

"OK," he answered, his ready smile receding.

Our story, Ramzi's and mine, sprouted from wherever it had been buried, without, I was surprised to find, having lost its texture.

Memories of the years I had spent next to him had been preserved in formaldehyde, complete with all the details I had unknowingly held on to. Even though Ramzi was no longer a presence in my life, our story progressed that night, beyond the story about him and me, or the love we had for each other. Now there was the memory of Sam and me talking about him. The memory of me sitting at my desk in London, writing about my recounting of this story to Sam. Another layer and another chapter, one that did not and would never again include him. It became my story and mine alone. I was its sole owner and could live with it as I wished.

Sam was quiet, attentive to my words. His eyes encouraged me to keep going as I spoke—unusually—without deception, without incomplete hints or hidden clues. I spoke until my past caught up with my present.

41

SAM'S lips lingered on mine the night he left after the end of term. *The heavens shake when two men lie with each other.* This was a warning from back home, omnipresent, menacing. Words written in the Quran, apparently, but I never bothered to check. The anecdote mattered more than the text.

My head had been resting on his thigh. He had lit a joint, and minutes ticked by in a flurry of smoke, drink, and laughs. I played a game in my head where I latched on to every minute that was attempting to float away, stopping each one from taking Sam, from hurtling me into a future I was unsure I could confront without him. I wondered if I would forsake Amman, and my family, to continue resting on his thigh. That night, our final together, it seemed a fair price to pay. Even with the weed, my chest tightened as the dawn edged closer. The weight on the couch shifted as he leaned over me. Time expanded, each second lasting more than a second. I smelled him just before his lips brushed against mine. Barely a kiss, more like a meeting of the lips. It was enough to confirm the Quran's warning. Everything in me trembled.

42

تجري الرياح بما لا تشتهي السفن—Mama would often repeat to herself. In that space between sleep and wakefulness, the tingle of his lips still on mine, after I had soaked his pillows with salt water, I understood. He had left some minutes, maybe hours, prior. The sound of the door shutting behind him rang in my ears as I lay wrapped in his duvet, the morning rays falling on my cheek. I traced the dust in the air, as I had done years before, lying behind Tata, trying to calm myself. To this day, the steps of a departing lover, the scent they leave behind, sinks me into an aching sadness. He was in my arms, his suitcase packed, then he was gone. The weight of the room, its silence, pressed down on me as the door clicked shut. I had walked to his bed, exhausted, pulled the covers back, and crawled in, smelling him on the pillows and in his sheets. I escaped, into my sleep, into a haze that lasted until the sun was in the middle of the sky.

The scale of the transformation that had happened in his room, between his ratty blue couch and his bed, settled into my body. Trying to suspend time and space by coming to Sydney had been futile. There was no future point at which I could begin to live the life I desired. Wanted or not, my life, the life I had been given, was in full swing; this was it.

Had I listened more closely, I might have understood Mama's words as she struggled to make sense of the way her own life had transpired: *The winds of the sea blow where the ships do not desire.* There is no way of controlling the winds, no point fighting the gales; one takes whatever fate blows their way. What that means, I think, is that all one can do is to build the sturdiest ship possible.

The alternative is to anchor down and wait for calmer seas, which so many of us have done in Amman. The bitterness that gnawed at me in Ramzi's wake is in those around me who are also cowed by our watchful societies; who barter the vastness of their dreams for the confines dictated by others; who limit their aspirations for fear of destabilizing small and petty souls. Ships moored in changing seas. I had seen the constrained life, most painfully, in Mama, who made herself smaller to fit into Amman. All those passing slights and immense injustices—from losing her comrades to Baba's insensitivities—she had gathered every one of those along the way, one on top of the other, keeping her embers stoked, a rebellion that had gone nowhere, consuming her from within. All the undignified insults we had to pretend we did not hear, the sacrifices we offered to satisfy others. The ways we had to make ourselves invisible to pass unnoticed. Who were we trying to please? Why, and for what purpose, did we limit ourselves in such a way?

And, as ever, there Ramzi was, looming over me as I lay in Sam's bed, making me lonelier than ever in the space that had just been vacated. I dozed off as that realization crystallized: No one, no matter how loved, even Ramzi, might have helped carry the load I had hauled alongside me. It was one of Ramzi's parting gifts: the knowledge that each of us is the sole bearer of our thoughts, the sole guardian of our inner selves. The distance between two people moving closer is never truly crossed. He was, I had to accept, no longer by my side. Sam had brought me, gently, to this realization.

That morning, absence was all around me. Gone were Ramzi's smirk and gray eyes. Gone was Sam from our nightly rituals. Neither of them to be seen again. Gone were the darting shadows, not in reality, but in the pricks they used to leave on my skin. Gone were the countless hours of remorse, and guilt, and the exhausting tyranny of denial. The only thing left was the self I had exiled, the life I had been avoiding. The sun's rays nudged me out of bed. I rose, leaving my past in Sam's bedsheets. I rose a ship floating in a black sea I did not yet know how to navigate. I walked toward the door Sam had departed from and made my way to my room, where packed suitcases were waiting to accompany me on my journey home.

43

AFTER Dr. Dajjani, I had thought myself endlessly brave, fighting for this vision of manhood I held dear, the one Ramzi represented. Through the years, he became a stand-in, a vague reference for everything I could not become. With no insight into the details of his life—how he woke up, what he was thinking, what he was bitching about, whether or not he was still smoking, what kind of person he had grown into—I had constructed a caricature of his man-ness. A banker. Living in the Gulf. A wife. I filled in blanks—and there were many—to make up the rest. But only one truth mattered: He was living the life my parents and I had hoped would one day be mine. If I was not like him, this thinking went, I did not belong back home.

But, having failed at becoming what I was so evidently not, what was I to be instead? I had lived in other people's realities for so long, I had lost sight of my own. After Sydney, I realized I was not free but lost, dazed by the prospect that there could be a path for me of my own making. I returned to London and its dark rooms. In gay saunas and hookup sites, I stepped into anonymity, into that space between invisibility and hypervisibility, as men cruise for sex shorn of all traits but their lust and body parts.

◆ ◆ ◆

When I finish university, I morph into a twenty-two-year-old corporate hire. Well-suited, numb in my work, awake in my body. Clubbing. Partying. Strobe lights flash on the dance floor. I look around, this time desperately. His eyes lock with mine, and between strokes of light, I see him walking over to where I stand, swaying uncomfortably on the side of the dance floor, tie loosened. He grabs it and pulls me in. No words are exchanged as his body clasps onto mine, like a key clicking neatly into its lock. His lips cover my mouth, eagerly, wetly, and I am alive. The music, my heartbeat, his shoulders—they all fuse together as I dissolve into my surroundings, elated. Every nerve in my body shoots up, ravenous, wanting this moment to go on and on.

Femi, a British-Nigerian model, settles into my life. We are novices, stumbling through the mechanics of sex, more concerned with the optics than the abandon. When Femi confesses his love, I run. Quit my job in London and move back to Amman—that fraught site of confrontation, where the old normal haunts me. I distract myself by spending time with Aya, a Saudi-Jordanian woman whose mane of hair smells of lavender. We sneak around the city, making out in my car in dark alleyways and fucking at home when Baba's snores signal safety. Another future flashes before my eyes and another swift exit.

In that same car—the burgundy Chevrolet with white leather interiors—I am again with William, crossing out of Syria into Lebanon, where I move for another job just after Israel's 2006 invasion. I look around, witness fresh scenes of destruction. The bridge we would have otherwise driven across to shorten our descent into Beirut from Chtaura has been blown up. Chunks of it dangle over the valley below, held back from freefall by disfigured and cluttered iron rods. I make this war-torn city my own, and meet Charbel, the catholic priest whose logic is as crooked as his cock. My lust is all-consuming, a proxy for a much bigger exorcism than I appreciate at the time. Desire burns until it fizzles, one night, when my masochism stares me in the face as he talks about counseling kids to atone for their gay thoughts. I leave after he tries to fuck me in his bare room at the monastery, where his crucifix hangs above his single bed.

◆ ◆ ◆

Clean slates can hold any narrative projected onto them. Slowly, I open myself up to desires held at bay and grow into the absences that had haunted my life. I begin to fashion a self into existence. Back in Amman, I smudge the city's white exteriors with everything that had been scrubbed off. I bring my perversions into this sanctimonious city. And in so doing, another question begins to haunt me: *What other silences have filled my childhood?*

44

THE room is sunken, with a window at eye level looking out onto the manicured gardens. I feel like a hedgehog, or one of my tortoises, peering into the grass from its cave. I am wrapped in the warmth of my blankets as I look outside. It is just past dawn, the sky pink. Frozen dew glistens in the haze. The spires of the college rise in the background. Another student room, bare, again below ground level. I am back in the UK, on a sabbatical from yet another unsatisfying job. I have enrolled in a postgraduate program in international relations, focused on the politics of the Middle East at Cambridge. I am seeking answers to the questions that continue to nag at me—about our lives, the spaces we grew up in, the cities that shaped us, the history that refuses to loosen its clutch on me. Next to my bed lies a stack of books about our region, its politics, our people. I wake up hours before class to read, wanting to satiate my curiosity, to learn what has been hidden from me, to swim in the undercurrents of my life.

It is cold and I want to stay in bed. But this morning, I have an early tutorial with a mentor. A giant of a scholar, the person who has become the vehicle for all the conversations I do not yet know how to have in Amman. In his first lecture, I sit next to a friend. The professor walks in between the aisles and up to his podium. He turns around, looks down at the class, and beams. My friend leans over. "Gosh, it's Santa Claus," she whispers. I giggle. It isn't just his white beard and protruding belly. It is his spirit. He is calm and gentle, with warm eyes and a paternal disposition. I know then that he is someone who will impart the knowledge that I crave, the guide who will help me uncover my family's history and reveal the details I know are missing from my childhood.

Weekly, I sit in his book-lined living room on a low brown leather couch. Flash, his terrier, cozies up next to me and proceeds to manically chew at his paws, a tic that persists throughout our work together, much to my mentor's agitation. "Flash," he would snap in a posh English accent, "you must stop!" He sits opposite me, with his white beard and crisp shirt. My papers, which he would have printed out and scribbled on, are spread in front of us. We barely look at those, their presence merely an excuse for expansive, meandering conversations. He is patient, rational, full of knowledge, as he takes me from Morocco to Algeria, Germany to Britain. We keep returning to Palestine, where, that year, 2007, Israel places Gaza under a cruel blockade. He is indignant, his blue eyes flashing with emotion, as he gives form to the injustice I have carried wordlessly within me my whole life. At some point in the conversation, Flash nuzzles my arm and moves it aside so he can nestle in my lap. My mentor jumps to his feet, and I assure him that this is a loved intrusion. We carry on. Evening sunlight streams through the windows as his study gradually morphs to resemble the balcony where my brothers and I would sit with Baba after his siestas, asking questions, prodding and challenging. Here, too, I come as a supplicant who is allowed to pretend he is an equal. I seek wisdom, and for whatever reason, he is generously willing to share it. He speaks of his own journey—a chemist turned historian—strengthening our kinship and allaying my fears of being an impostor in this field, where I have arrived woefully underprepared. He assures me that this history lives in my body, and, with a father's kindness, he assumes the responsibility of helping me unearth it.

In that room over countless afternoons, I slowly weave together the strands of narrative, spoken and emoted, that had shaped my life. All the stories of heroism and wartime that my brothers and I had grown up with are reassembled, given place and time and context. All the pain that I had been previously unable to hear is held, witnessed. The knowledge of our history—until then vague, shallow, Haifa and Beirut merely distant pasts to our present—is deepened. I learn I had been living in another kind of shadow, another kind of silence. Palestine was present all around us in Amman, but was she really seen? She was everywhere and nowhere all at once.

I never miss those sessions. I glance up at the frosty lawn, brave the cold, and roll out of bed, bare feet on the carpet, and make my way to the bathroom down the hall. I squeeze into the standing shower and begin washing my hair. I have barely warmed up, shampooing as I think about my tutorial that morning. Much is happening in Palestine and Gaza—Gaza, Gaza—is being erased. That is where my mind keeps returning to, my research questions beginning to take form through the exchange between the two of us. As my mind wanders, a thought surfaces that startles me. On this icy morning, I have made it this far without thinking of Ramzi. Whole minutes between rising and groggily getting into that shower. *Seven years*, I count in my head. It has been seven years from that call to him not being the first thing I think about when I wake up.

♦ ♦ ♦

After my sabbatical ends, I decide that I want more. I sign on to a doctoral program with my supervisor, though I also return to work to pay for my studies. I make London my base, moving into a small studio in Hammersmith. Every month, on the train to his house, I fret about the state of the chapters I have submitted. My work is demanding, my travel hectic, and I am barely able to keep up with my coursework, sending him half-baked thoughts and flimsily constructed arguments. But then he opens the door and offers the same remark, as if it were the most surprising thing in the world. "You're right on time, Tareq, not a minute later than our appointment!"

Between those sessions, I flit from Europe to the Middle East and back, unwilling to settle in either, noncommittally living in both. Week after week, I board a plane from London to Saudi Arabia, Bahrain, the UAE, Qatar, or Oman, where my clients live. I spend weekends in Amman or Beirut, with friends and family. Before I leave London, I pack as many books as I can fit into my carry-on, from left-wing ideologues to Islamist preachers and queer memoirs. I am engaged in a conversation with my mentor that is uninterrupted, flowing against the backdrop of endless travel. These are books that are absent from my home and, while crossing security points at airports, they burn in my bag, unwelcome under the gaze of security officers. I start to take off their book jackets so they can pass undetected. And in the spaces of the commute, on planes and in terminals, I read.

On flights to Saudi Arabia, when we reach somewhere east of the Mediterranean, the atmosphere in the cabin shifts. The women put on their headscarves, pull their abayas over their bodies. I go into the bathroom, change out of my skinny jeans into a well-tailored suit. I take my seat, put my books away. In our cities, my mask is a familiar companion, donned and taken off as needed, allowing me to occupy a role so familiar it is no longer a performance. On those trips, darting shadows flirt with desire, steering me into spaces I had thought nonexistent. Where a glance around the pool of my hotel in Riyadh would have flushed me with shame, it turns into a sweaty encounter in the middle of the day. Where a straitlaced party in Manama would have offered little to hold my interest, erotic exchanges happen just below the surface.

Nothing is as it presents, and those fronts—unwelcome, suffocating—lose their power over me. I learn to look behind their whitewashed facades to find the universes tucked away in shadows within our cities. In those spaces, I come back into my skin, fucking Arab men who despise their queerness and queer men who despise their Arabness, and a whole range in between. Men who, like me, are navigating the tensions held in the containers of their bodies. I learn that the dogs in Dr. Dajjani's metaphor are alive and well, fucking for anger, fucking for self-loathing, fucking for both. And, in their own ways, living and loving.

Home becomes less menacing. The athaan affirms a belonging that is lacking in London. The airless heat offers comfort. The sounds of our cities—trucks selling gasoline canisters, incessant honking, humming diesel engines and touring food carts—punctuate all conversations, melodiously affirming my return. And the food: I relish the freshness of the mezes and the salads and the heartiness of the meats, the bread, the rice, with a desire for physical and spiritual nourishment. I love the way the sand tickles my feet on marble tiles, the coolness of the white stone walls, the shade that engulfs me when I walk in from the glaring sunlight—all sensations that take me home to al-Abdali, to the patio I crossed every day to play with my tortoises. Amman and Beirut, even Riyadh and Manama, become—once again—my centers of gravity.

And in London, too, a metamorphosis is under way. When I left for university, I pushed back against Mama's efforts to fill my suitcases with spices and foods and incense. "You will not find any of your favorite meals there," she warned. *Precisely the point*, I thought. Ties had to be severed. Now, a tumultuous love affair began. Memories exploded in my mind from corners they had long been packed away in. Cinnamon, Naguib Mahfouz, and Majida El Roumi crept into my daily life. I rediscovered the poems of Nizar Qabbani and the writings of Ghassan Kanafani. I devoured Arabic novels I bought in Beirut's alleyways to make up for lost time and reentered the folds of my mother tongue, realizing it was a more intuitive fit than this foreign one. Disjointed memories of Baba sitting in the darkness, listening to Umm Kulthum, popped into my mind during crushed morning commutes. Fairuz blasted into my headphones while I walked along the Thames, taking me to scenes long locked away.

When I wasn't traveling to the region, and had run out of vacuum-packed thyme, I raided Syrian markets in Shepherd's Bush. I scouted all the grocery stores, looking for produce; those with the best مناقيش and the ones with the most workable طحينة. My fridge began resembling the one I grew up peering into, with tubs of labneh and slabs of halloumi. I learned to cook my favorite meals, massaging chicken with sumac, olive oil, and pine nuts for مسخن and piling layers of deep-fried eggplant with stewed lamb cubes and rice for مقلوبة. My kitchen smelled like ours in al-Abdali when Mama's cooking nudged me out of sleep before dawn.

Every Sunday, before my grocery run, I called Tata. After assuring her that I was going to church and praying for forgiveness, I would implore her to talk to me about recipes. Initially, I had to endure her doubts.

"Why can't you find a nice Arab girl to cook for you? You work so hard. You come from work dead tired—you deserve to have a hot meal waiting for you."

I eventually wore her down.

"You should lightly fry the ملوخية leaves with garlic before you add the meat and water for it to stew."

"Do شوربة العدس on cold nights. It's very easy: just lentils and some cumin, and let it boil for an hour. Remember to soak the lentils overnight!"

"Leave the كوسا for us here, it takes too long and it's too much kitchen work for a young man."

Some boundaries had to be drawn.

◆ ◆ ◆

On one trip to Riyadh, after a long day of meetings, I was too tired to settle into my evening study ritual at the hotel. I left my room and walked out into the dusty, hot night, hailing a cab to take me downtown, where I could walk around without being surrounded by traffic. Markets were open, and it was early enough that many pedestrians were out after a day of being locked indoors to avoid the heat. I walked like I knew where I was going, passing by argileh cafés filled with men and Western fast-food outlets teeming with teenagers. I walked aimlessly until I stumbled upon the domineering walls of the Ministry for the Propagation of Virtue and Prevention of Vice. A grand white building with words written on its front in beautiful, black Arabic calligraphy. There, I stopped.

I sat on a sidewalk in its courtyard, where beheadings and lashings occasionally take place, and watched people going about their business, enjoying the relief from the day's sun. *Who gets to walk on those streets, and who gets excised from them?* Despite the market activity, the courtyard appeared to me forlorn. The streetlights were a heavy yellow and the tall metal gates of the ministry unwelcoming. The courtyard itself was paved with stone slabs that reminded me of those that dotted the oval forum at the entrance to Jerash's ancient city. My coworkers at the time, most of whom were foreign, had attended some of the public trials, feeding their orientalist fantasies of Eastern savagery. I had not joined; the site haunted me, not because of its barbarism, but because of how viscerally I understood it. It was the natural extension, the logical culmination, of the darting shadows.

From unthinking glances to guillotines. The ministry is the mortar-and-brick incarnation of everything Ramzi railed against in our cocoon. All that we thought stifled us—*3eib* and honor and religion and nationalism—is built into that monolith, with its imposing facade and angry exterior. Foolishly, as I sat looking at the entrance outside, I felt powerful, as if in its presence I could dismantle everything it stood for. It became pitiful, its medievalism transforming it into a caricature, a parody of itself. I got up feeling lighter and walked away. That night, I played close to its steps, mocking the small men and women who see virtue in its stones.

45

I TOLD Mama about Ramzi—again—on the top floor of a double-decker bus. She was visiting me in London, and it had become clear shortly after her arrival that she was visiting with an agenda. Huddled in the autumn cold, on the upper deck of the bus back from the Tate Modern to my flat, we picked up where we left off after Dr. Dajjani. "Listen to me, my son," she said. "I do not want to lecture you nor to tell you what to do. But I have a mother's instinct: I hurt when you hurt, and I can tell you're hurting. Talk to me," she begged, "confide."

Along the 19 route, as the bus passed Green Park, I did—this time with authority. I introduced her to who I had become, talked to her about the margins I was living in. Explained that while I did not have all the answers, I knew not to make myself smaller to fit the ones I had been given. She said nothing and listened attentively, nodding. Then she started asking questions—ones that were calm, collected, as if she had long prepared herself for this exchange. *How long have you known? Have you been holding this secret since Dr. Dajjani? Why didn't you come talk to me?* Questions that skirted around the confession itself, tracing its implications, not yet its substance. When we got off the bus, she hugged me. *She would teach me how to rage with dignity*, I thought, *how to rage without burning myself and others down*. Maybe together, we could make light of our shared bitterness. Almost immediately, we began plotting how we would tell Baba, this time not to seek his advice, but to give ours.

That night, Ramzi was in my dreams. Young and beautiful and dressed in white, he had not aged one bit in the years since I had seen him. I did not have a sense of myself in the dream, whether I was older or the teenager I was when he had known me. I was dressed in white as well. We were stretched out on a bed—Tata's bed in Amman—our bodies intertwined. We were kissing, our hands resting on each other, casually, as though that did not defy all possibility, like it could be taken for granted. There was very little that mattered beyond us, and I was entirely engrossed in him, in that moment and in his body. The dream was more blissful than erotic. There within his arms was where I needed to be. My body was almost giddy with the sense of rightness that rarely manifests outside the dream world, living a moment that was exciting and unknown and full of beauty.

A noise outside my bedroom window yanked me out of that rapturous haze. I rested in the space between sleep and consciousness. I was no longer with Ramzi. I was floating through clouds that parted to show Mama, standing opposite me. There was nothing dramatic in our encounter, no anger or resentment, but a question, a query in my bones, one that was felt rather than articulated. How could she and everyone around me, but her especially, not have seen the wonder around those two bodies entangled in white? Tears moistened my pillow. It was an unkind dream, taunting me with the possibility of what could have been.

♦ ♦ ♦

Close to two decades later, I ask Mama about that bus ride. *What did I say, exactly? How did I phrase things? How did she feel?* She remembers the conversation like it was yesterday, she tells me. Every word, every gesture. Pictures of scribbled notes land on my phone after I hang up with her. Notes she wrote on hotel stationery that night after I had taken her back to her room. Words like *scared, bewildered, confused* swim around on the screen of my iPhone. Blame: *How could this have happened? Was I not attentive enough as a mother?* And confrontation: *He had always been so depressed as a child, aloof and quiet, how had I not known? How had I not been able to hear earlier?* Reading her words on-screen, on a technology that was not available at the time of our chat, reminds me of how much time has elapsed, of how long our journeys have taken.

♦ ♦ ♦

Unbeknownst to me, Mama decided to drug Baba with a sedative on the night we planned to tell him, a few months after that bus ride. Baba was the final frontier. And even though I still had unanswered questions, I knew that he, too, had to be faced without doubts. He would pounce on the slightest waver in my voice, and re-burden me with all the expectations I had painstakingly shed—am still shedding. There was a need for a definitiveness I was unsure I had. I armed myself for hurtful accusations; it had taken me years to come to terms with myself, so I anticipated his need for time.

On the planned day, in Amman, I returned home at dusk and walked up the stairs. The breeze came in from the open balcony door, carrying tunes from Baba's portable radio. I looked at his back as a thin plume of smoke rose from his cigar, swirling above his head. Mama was making his coffee in the kitchen. She smiled and gave me a determined nod. There was no turning back. She had been nervous about my telling Baba, anticipating conflict. "Does he have to know?" she started asking, fearing this would break the family. In Baba's fits of rage—far more infrequent than Mama's, but, in their rarity, devastating—things could be said that would be difficult to unsay. She also knew there was no other option.

My limbs were shaky. Adrenaline seeped through my veins. The balcony was entirely unchanged from the way it had looked that night, a few days after my last call with Ramzi. Baba, too, rested in exactly the same position, with the camel robe wrapped around his shoulders. I sat on the chair that had held me before, with the same black smudges on the white plastic.

"طروقة العظيم," he sang.

My eyes welled up. I wondered when I would hear those words again. Baba was oblivious to this turmoil, gazing somewhere in the distance, listening to the news, sipping his coffee. He was quiet.

"Baba, I love you," I started.

"I love you, too," he said reflexively. "What's wrong?"

"Baba, I need to talk to you." He put his mug down and turned to me. I continued. "What I'm about to tell you is not easy for me. And I need you to listen to what I have to say before getting angry. OK?"

"Baba, you're worrying me. Tell me what's wrong."

"Nothing's wrong, Baba. Remember when I came to you, right here on this balcony, years ago? I had just had a fight with Ramzi, and I told you things were confusing, and I was worried that I was attracted to boys. I didn't know what that meant, and you said it was normal, a phase, it would pass."

He nodded.

"I believed you. And for years, even when I had doubts, I wanted to believe you. I tried. I dated girls. Tried to grow out of it. But Baba, I'm here to tell you that it was not a phase. And I'm OK with that. Baba, I am gay. I've known for years; I was just not ready to accept it. This is who I am."

Words tumbled out in quick succession, in fear that I would be cut off before I could deliver all my thoughts in coherent order. I wanted to show resolve, but in my haste there was nervousness, and a desire to comfort him, to help him see beyond that word, *gay*, which would evoke the same feeling of repulsion I had felt when Ramzi offered it to me.

He was no longer looking at me. He was back in the distance. The radio had moved on to the news. He said nothing, and I sat there, thankful, and frightened. Thankful that instead of rage there seemed to be some reflection. And frightened about exactly that. I waited, resisting the urge to puncture the bubble, yet feeling unprepared for what might come next.

"Cambridge did this to you," he finally said, after interminable minutes had passed.

"What?"

"Cambridge did this to you. That's why I never wanted you to go study in London and then in Cambridge. I knew they would put ideas in your head. This is not Cambridge, Tareq. That is not our world. You think that you can come back and say things like this, and what, people will accept it? You see how they live in Cambridge and you think you can also have the same thing here?"

"Baba, I've been having these thoughts since I was ten."

"People will not accept this here. We're backward. We're not like you or your friends in Cambridge. This is a different world. You cannot live here anymore."

I did not respond. After a few minutes, he continued, speaking slowly, drowsily, as he delivered a determined verdict.

"You must promise me two things, Baba. You will never come back to live here. You have to build your home in London now." He paused, waiting for me to object. When nothing was forthcoming, he went on. "And you will never tell your brothers about any of this."

"What? Why?"

"Baba, they will not understand. I do not want to see this family break up because of something you're deciding to do. This will not be accepted. And I don't want that kind of pressure on them."

Post-news music played in the background, incongruously light. Baba gazed to a far-off place. The air between us was heavy with the reverberations of the sounding shot he had fired. There was nothing left to say at this point. He turned to me as I stood up to go back inside.

"I wish you never told me, Tareq. When they put me in my coffin not so long from now, this will be my only regret in life, the one thing I wish could be different. And I wish you had the decency to let me die not knowing you were like this."

V

46

BACK in London, an email changes the course of my life. *It's only an academic introduction,* my friend quips, easing my doubts about her offer to put me in touch with a graduate student she knows. *If nothing else, you can exchange notes on your doctoral research.* Her email is casual, light, reducing each of us to a two-line bio before urging us to meet. *I leave the rest to you . . .* she teases at the end. On cue, a correspondence begins—tentatively, electronically. No letters to be archived in the yellow box. Instead, emails that land in my inbox with increasing frequency. Hesitant explorations of interest, curious trawling around digital footprints across the ocean; him in New York, me in London. Emails that expand into lengthy missives and that, soon after they begin, arrange for us both to be in Beirut for a summer. A correspondence that intertwines our separate lives across oceans into an enduring, unexpected, incredible conversation. An archive of togetherness that would, years later, expand to hold memories of a wedding and a life in London, one that is still being assembled.

VI

47

اتعرفين ما هو الوطن يا صفية؟—Ghassan Kanafani's protagonist turns to his wife and asks, at one point in *Returning to Haifa*. They are standing in their Haifa home, from which they had fled in 1948 and returned to that evening in 1967, days after Israel's occupation of the rest of Palestine began. Before Israel's military regime had perfected the tactics of sieving Palestinians out, one could still travel the short distance from the West Bank to Haifa on impulse. They found themselves standing in their former sitting room, speaking to the house's current residents, an elderly Jewish woman and the protagonist's son, an army officer, whom the Jewish woman had raised as her own, as an Israeli man. Any leftover sense of the officer's Palestinian-ness—maybe the words of a lullaby his parents had sung to him before Haifa fell, before the panic of that day tore their family apart—had vanished. Dispelled so that nothing stirred within him, not even when looking at Palestinians through the sight of his rifle during his army service in the occupied territory, or at his parents, standing opposite him as strangers, as unwelcome intruders. The vacuum left behind, the one that had been filled by another homeland, a Zionist homeland, had prompted that question from the main character—*Do you know what a homeland is?*—as the protagonist and his wife grappled with understanding what they had gone back in time and space to reclaim: Their home? Their child? Their history?

I stand at the check-in desk in Heathrow and hand over my passport, barely a few days old, acquired after years living in the UK. The red of its cover is unfamiliar between my fingers; I have not yet adjusted to being designated a British citizen. I look at the check-in agent, half expecting her to tell me that there has been a mistake; red passport or not, I am still Palestinian, and therefore, I am still not allowed to fly to

Palestine. I hold my breath. The 2014 Israeli assault on the Gaza Strip has just ended. There is nowhere else I want to go with my newfound freedom. I exhale only when she asks me if I want an aisle or window seat. *Colonialism is heredity*, I think to myself, *with domination passing from one great power to the next, and subjugation from one subject to their offspring.* This red passport in my hand is a permission slip offered by my grandparents' colonial power, Britain, to enter through the securitized gates of my colonial master, Israel.

Before I have even boarded my flight to Al-Lydd Airport—now named after the architect of the Nakba, David Ben-Gurion—I am already recoiling from the quotidian life of Israeli society. There is the mother who is exasperated her baby will not stop crying. There is the elderly couple returning from their trip abroad—to see their grandchildren in the UK, I imagine. A class of schoolkids fills the gate area, watched over by their teachers. Staff and students are wearing bright blue T-shirts, the blue and white of the Israeli flag, with a chirpy quote that reads "Israel: Imagine the Places You'll Go!" The words are plastered onto the map of Palestine. I put on my headphones and open my book. I get lost in reading for the duration of the flight, but my nerves are frayed with anticipation by the time I land.

Eight hours after my arrival in the airport, after what I will come to understand is the customary humiliation and interrogation of Palestinians by Israeli agents—"Does your father know you're gay?" one plainclothes officer asks me in a back room I have been escorted to. "Yes," I answer, my voice steely cold and at odds with my churning insides. "Would you like his number?"—I make it into the baggage reclaim and arrivals. Here, too, signs of ordinary life abound. I look up at the colorful balloons stuck in the ceiling of the airport's reception hall. I visualize them flying off from a loved one's hand as she hugs her lover on arrival. There is the man who has driven out to welcome his family and who is enjoying an espresso on the bar of the Aroma Café. The mundane, thoroughly tepid manifestations of Israeli life, the same as any society's, aggrieve me. How can there be normality amidst the absurd?

These days, Mama is quieter, smaller somehow, as if she has finally—after decades—accepted the role she has been offered. The fire of her rebellion, burning madly before, appears to have been doused. I used to think it was because she had become resigned or had been defeated, accepting—like Baba—that her rage will not lead to change. It took me a long time to understand that is not the case. Our struggle, too, is hereditary. Mama has taught me that. She has simply passed on the baton, the one she had been given from Tata, who had received it from her mother.

◆ ◆ ◆

Having never visited the land, on arrival, I understood that I had grown up there. In al-Abdali, like in the rest of Amman, Palestine thrives, unnamed, between our four walls: in our sensibility, our ache, our politics, our collective memories, our desires. It is in the accent of the people, the architecture of our homes and our gardens, in the smells of our kitchens and our bedtime stories. Walking throughout Palestine, I was haunted by the specter of a past community and recalled lives I never lived, in a lost world that had been passed on to me through Tata's love.

No, not lost; stolen.

Al-Abdali had prepared me to detect its silent presence, trained my eyes to fill in the blanks that Tata had left unspoken. The white-dotted bushes that she pointed to in our garden in Amman filled my nostrils with their fragrance in Haifa, where I searched, seven decades later, looking for a house, her house, while mourning the scattered lives of the inhabitants of all the other houses, now filled with Jewish strangers.

In this quest, people urged me to move on. "Palestine is gone," an old Palestinian woman, easily Tata's age, told me on a street corner in Haifa one afternoon when I asked her about Tata's house. "Your grandparents are gone, and so is Palestine. Let go, my son," she said gently, "there is nothing for you to find here." She could not see Palestine all around her. Masked behind the European-looking buildings and the proclaimed Western sensibility, beneath the Hebrew street names and modern architecture, Palestine lies, present, dormant. Hiding herself, passing undetected against the backdrop of the Israeli society that had planted itself in her midst. Within the most private dwellings stand Palestinian walls bearing witness. Beneath the distractions of the settler nation, Palestine is everywhere, in its crevices and alleyways, in its topography, in its splendid stone mansions, grand municipal buildings, and cemeteries adorned with bougainvillea and olive trees and jutting minarets. Palestine remains where she has always been, its skeleton erect and dignified, waiting, even as the flesh around it—foreign, hostile—expands in its emptied quarters.

I peer into the doorways of house after house in Haifa, having traversed a different time and an altogether different space than Kanafani's protagonist, back to a site of rupture that had been entombed within my chest. I open Tata's diaries. This time, I am less interested in the years after the Nakba. I turn to the beginning. The pages documenting the days prior to 1948 are short. Most of her life had transpired elsewhere: Beirut, Amman. Stints in Damascus and Riyadh. Before calamity, one does not imagine its possibility, and her words in those early pages reflect a world that is entirely unimaginable from this side. In keeping with her style, the pages are sparse in number and description—no more than twenty, with no musings or daydreams—just the facts of life narrated around her. Echoes of names I hear in Amman. Each page comes to life, dances before my eyes, fills with movement. So-and-so cousin died of a brain aneurysm in Haifa. That one's sister passed away in Jerusalem—she was far too young. He became betrothed to a woman from the Tarazi family—the Gaza branch. She married a man from Nazareth. This one moved to Haifa. That one lived in al-Baqa'a al-Fawqha in Jerusalem. This one went to Cairo for work, that one to Damascus to study.

I imagine Tata's family dressing up and going to someone's wedding in Jaffa, or a funeral in Jerusalem. This one graduating here, that one having a baby girl there. Traversing the country, from Nazareth to Gaza, falling in love, going on summer breaks to Ramallah. Dwelling in those pages, Palestine comes to life around me. I can see Tata returning from school. Witness her father donning his frock and going to Mass. Smell the cooking her mother prepared in the kitchen every day.

Their move from Jerusalem to Haifa was one I could make myself now. Drive from Jerusalem's hills down to the coast, see Mount Carmel peek at me from the distance as I drive up to the port.

Tata had no way of knowing how her writing would be read seven decades later. That is what gives these pages their power. Continuity was taken for granted. One could inhabit the mundane, not the catastrophic. The fabric that held this place together has been ripped apart. There is a wholesomeness to her words, an innocence that slices through me as I read, seeing what could have been. Witnessing someone who lived through and experienced this country, its rich community, its interconnectedness to the region, to Amman and Cairo. There was enmeshment here, beauty and ugliness, joy and mourning, humanity.

What have the Zionists done?

I, of course, knew the answer to that question very well. My work with my mentor had armed me with the knowledge I needed for this trip. But when I stood in Jerusalem, this city that had loomed large in my family's imagination, that knowledge was barely a consolation. Amman was less than a hundred kilometers to the east, Gaza a taxi ride away. Neither of them reachable without crossing racist walls. The gossip filling Tata's diaries felt like the work of fiction, the prose of a master storyteller.

❖ ❖ ❖

My husband and I are having breakfast with a retired Palestinian urban planner who had built his career in Haifa's municipality and developed a reputation for mapping the city's streets. Clandestinely, of course; he was, after all, a Palestinian in the heart of Israel's bureaucracy. Here is a man able to juxtapose Haifa's contemporary landscape with the blueprints of the city in 1948, on the edge of calamity, as it remains frozen in time in the minds of all the Nakba survivors who were expelled. Flocks of Palestinians come to him, hoping that he can—magically—take them back in time and make sense of the vaguest directions that have been passed down from their dying elders. I have come to him with the same such vagueness.

"ليش يا ابني؟" Tata implored when I first told her, on a call from London, that I was traveling to Palestine. "Why do you want to go there?" she asked. I talked her through her fears and into her hopes, untouched for decades, that it is our right to return, that this injustice that had plagued her will not remain a silent, unwanted companion. I reminded her that Mama, too, had made this journey, and that every generation in our family will claim this right until it is secured. Just like with her recipes, gentle prodding undid her hesitation. "Go to the Italian Hospital," she told me. "Keep it on your right-hand side. Turn right just before you get to the actual hospital. From there, it's the first left and second right. Our house is the one on the corner closest to the sea. A two-story villa." I had no street name or house number; she could recall neither. *Is there any point walking in the backstreets behind the hospital?*

"There is," our urban planner tells us, handing us books about Haifa's topography. That area has not been leveled and little has changed. The plot sizes and street names have all been altered, obviously, but the general skeleton of the area has been preserved. "Just follow her directions," he says, "and see where you find yourself." We thank him and set off. The midday sun beats down on us as we walk along the busy main road away from Haifa's main strip and toward the Italian Hospital. It's hot and I'm anxious. We have spoken about this before, my husband and I. There might be a chance that the house will never be found. But that is, in some ways, a more straightforward outcome than finding it. Because what then? Will I knock on its front door? Will I ask to see it? What if the house is inhabited by an Israeli family, or worse, an American Jewish family just summering there, holding Tata's home hostage to their vacations? Will they be aggressive if I introduce myself as the original occupant's grandson? What will they make of us, bursting into the middle of their day, asserting belonging, living proof of crimes they have inherited and abetted?

No clear answers have been reached by the time we come up to a building that our phones tell us is the Italian Hospital. Neither of us says anything as we take the right just before the hospital and walk down to the street behind it. First left. The area is quiet, with none of the highway traffic spilling over. The streets are wide and olive trees are planted on the sidewalks. We could be in Amman or Beirut. The houses are mostly villas or small residential buildings, two or three stories, all limestone, strangely familiar, except for the Hebrew lettering on the front doors and the mezuzahs hanging in the entrances.

Second right. We walk down in the direction of the sea. We get to the first crossing, and the house on the other side of the street, closest to the sea, is a two-story villa. The front gates are shut—black metal—and there is an unwieldy jasmine bush spilling over its walls and lining its entrance. It's a narrow pathway to the front door—a brown wooden frame that appears shut. The second-floor windows are shuttered. I instinctively turn and look diagonally across the street. A grand villa. The one that had acquired a forlorn look in the weeks before Tata's flight, where her best friend had lived, from where her family had fled, furtively in the middle of the night, to Tata's dismay.

I look back at Tata's house, smaller than her friend's, now haloed with new importance. My husband grabs my hand, wordlessly. He knows. I know. We've heard her descriptions. Neither of us needs to say anything. I cross the street and stand by the gate, taking in the scent in the air, looking up at what I imagine was her bedroom. Where she was sitting when her father rushed back in, panicked, on that fateful night. She must have stood exactly where I am standing now and turned around for that final glance, suitcase in hand. *Is this the same jasmine bush? Can it be?* My mind fixates on this—the bush, its roots, its size. *Do jasmine trees live this long? How old would it be now, seven decades later?* My eyes turn back to the house. It looks uninhabited. Or maybe they've just left for the day, whoever *they* are. What has this house seen in the decades between her and me standing in this spot? What had *she* seen, other than a lifetime of flight?

My chest tightens and I take a step back. I cannot bring myself to ring the doorbell. There is only so much loss one can bear. I do not want to know, do not want to be faced with a family that believes it has a right to be there, or worse, a kind family that acknowledges this past, and then offers us a drink in my home. I want to imagine it empty, loyal, waiting for our return. I want it to exist outside of time, as if everything stopped that April. *Their presence or absence is irrelevant,* I tell myself. This is about her, about Tata, about me stepping through that fracture that ran along this entrance, physically reconnecting our histories. I have finally bent time, held her history in my present. I walk to the other side of the street and take a picture. I send it to Mama. *I think I found it*, I write in the caption. She responds immediately. *This looks like everything she's described. Where did you find it? How come I couldn't?* she writes back. And then, a few seconds later: *I'm glad she doesn't have the eyesight to see it now.*

48

A FEW days after I find Tata's house, I am dropped off at the Beit Hanoun crossing, the main entry point to the Gaza Strip, where I plan to spend time doing fieldwork, immersed in an excavation that is as much personal as it is scholarly. I bring out the paperwork that has taken months to arrange so I can cross this boundary—erected precisely to prevent Palestinians from returning to their stolen homes, from doing what I myself am doing. It is a domineering terminal, made up of the building blocks of prison complexes—wires and metal gates—reinforced with highly digitized systems of control. I walk in through the large gray entryway and into a hall that looks like an airport check-in lounge. At the counter, a young blond woman sits behind thick glass. I hand her my paperwork, answer all her questions, both the administrative and the intrusive, and after some time am allowed in. One can easily be exiled, banished into oblivion; it is the return journey that is fraught.

I am unprepared. The Palestine I was uncovering in Haifa lies in tatters before me. This strip, a tiny sliver on the southernmost part of our homeland, is a testament to their desire to rewrite history, to render absent what is so evidently present and alive. I roam all over, conscious of how little time I have been given, resentful that I need permission to be here in the first place. The same evening that I enter Gaza, I make my way to Beit Hanoun in the north, just south of the so-called border I had crossed. This is one of the sites most heavily bombarded in the 2014 assault, which had ended a few months prior, and the area amounts to little more than mounds of rubble. I walk around, taking it in, overwhelmed by rage—Mama's rage, red hot, persistently simmering in the background, bubbles up—and climb one of the mountains of debris. I look across the fence toward the other side.

Orderly white houses are arranged in rows, separated by groomed trees and well-manicured front lawns. I can see a bus crossing through Sderot, an Israeli colony built on the ruins of Najd, and visualize young children being ferried back and forth from school, getting off the bus and rushing into the smell of their grandmothers' cooking. "They have made Palestine European," Mama had said after her own journey back. It did indeed look European, and by this I mean misplaced, incongruent in its surroundings. But that is not the thought that pops into my mind as I look over the fence. I think of how well that wholesome facade deflects the gaze of its inhabitants from ugly truths, ones powerful enough to unravel their whole fantasy of make-believe; that this pretty, European-looking city—nation—is built on death and destruction and sustained by nothing more than colonial racism.

In Gaza, there are no polished facades. No corner of our past is left untouched by the settlers' cruelty, their arrogance and fear: it is all on full display here. One lives the truth of what humanity has done—is doing—and in that honesty, there is pain, but also freedom. Refugee camps dissolve into the urban space around them, overcoming any distinction between camp and city, the past not severed behind walls, but living instead in the present. Throughout my time here, I walk through spaces that I come to love even while wishing they never existed. Narrow alleyways snaking between tiny homes. Small shopfronts with basic goods and household supplies. School children running around or sitting on doorsteps with their Tatas. Graffiti that honors our history—documenting everything left unsaid in my white city, back in Amman—is painted all over the walls of the camps. Murals of keys awaiting return alongside poems of resistance for fighters. Palestinian flags adorn alleyways, and pictures of martyrs are plastered all over, layers upon layers of loss and sacrifice. These camps might as well have been the same ones I visit in Beirut, the ones Mama had grown up frequenting. Sites that are full of life, emerging after that rupture in 1948, suspended in time in their quest for justice.

My days are packed with interviews, meetings, and archival visits. In the evenings, I go to the pier, where people congregate by the water, barbecuing, eating, swimming. I sit with friends—cherished connections I have made over the course of my studies, and with whom I have corresponded across the barriers, others to whom I've been introduced during this visit—and the way they speak surprises me. I find no signs of the heaviness I carry around with me. Even though we talk about the darkness of their reality, of the politics of living under apartheid, they cling to a lightness, to a celebration of life, to humor. It is an absence that reminds me of Baba and Mama, of their Beirut, of the beauty of their lives unfolding even amidst war and destruction. Of the stubbornness of living even with the constant reminders of dying. How awe-inspiring that is, and how unjust. In Gaza, none of the pretenses that I have grown up with exist. Amman's white facades are replaced with a realness that is difficult to behold, one that awakens the soul. I fall in love and begin to understand that this tiny sliver of land holds the secrets to our world.

◆ ◆ ◆

What do I mean by this—*holds the secrets to our world*? Gaza is the abject of our time. A miserable stretch of land, overpopulated and dirty, drowning in its own shit and decrepit infrastructure, beaten and abused. In the Israeli collective psyche, Gaza is a dark place, full of terrorists, of angry hordes, a place where—in the words of a former minister of justice, no less—Palestinian mothers give birth to snakes, not babies. In our popular imagination, Gaza is ugly, cut off from the world, demonized, pitied, misunderstood, disgusting, besieged. I could dismiss all this rhetoric—write here that the Gaza I visited burst with energy, that its cafés were full of young, inspiring people, that its markets bustled and its cars idled in traffic. But anything I write would sound desperate in the very act of articulation; such is the power of dominant narratives.

So, I will write only this: The power of the abject is revolutionary, and because of that, immense resources are invested in ensuring it remains invisible or is otherwise rendered repulsive. It is precisely Gaza's abjection that makes it the site of revolution, a land teeming with life and love, a territory with the power to shake our world out of its stupor. I am not romanticizing the misery in Gaza—far from it. What I am trying to convey is that in the most abject of spaces, in the queerest of selves, beauty abounds. Gaza does not stand alone in this. What she taught me is that sights unseen, words unspoken, realities despised, contain our most essential truths, our most precious meaning. What power can be harnessed if our sites of abjection are embraced, brought out in the open, the sores of vilification healed. That is where our liberation lies.

◆ ◆ ◆

Entry into Gaza is far swifter than exit, I find out after my precious time there. Red blinking lights and loudspeakers direct the trickle of travelers who are privileged enough to leave their imprisonment through a dizzying maze. Long corridors are interspersed with bare rooms furnished with cold steel tables over which Palestinians are forced to shed their clothes and open their luggage. Israeli administrators look down at these subjects through bulletproof glass cubicles one floor above, as if through a microscope. Human interaction has been efficiently scrubbed out, and communication reduced to lights and automated instructions. As I stand opposite an Israeli security agent manning the last counter after this labyrinth, before I am allowed to "reenter" Israel, I recall just how banal evil can be.

49

I MOVED to a wintery Palestine a few years later. I arrived in Ramallah during a bitter and wet November and rented a spacious, sparsely furnished flat let out by Aida, a kind older woman with whom I immediately forged a friendship as we re-created the other in the image of faraway loved ones. She was my Tata in Palestine and I was a stand-in for her grandchildren, grown and living abroad. Every few days, I would pick her up and we would go grocery shopping in Ramallah al-Tahta. "This grocer stocks Israeli produce," she would caution, "and this one is overpriced." She would lead me to her go-to places and, like Tata, huff at the fact that I was cooking my own meals. At her insistence, I would frequently go to her home for lunch, and she would regale me with stories.

Her family had fled Jaffa in 1948 and settled in Ramallah, where—like many affluent Jaffa families—they had long summered. Over the decades, Ramallah morphed from a quaint summer village into a gilded cage, a city that resembled Amman with its polished facades and sense of make-believe—in this case, that Ramallah was not a city under military occupation. Here, unlike in Gaza, apartheid is sanitized. As long as one turns a blind eye to night raids and avoids checkpoints, one can imagine an occupation-free existence. "The younger people have forgotten," Aida would say in dismay. "That is why I write." Children's books illustrated with fetching characters adorned her study, where she narrated Palestine in its simplest terms, dispelling all efforts to render it complicated. "Even children—especially children—understand," she would tell me.

Whereas I came to her with stories of exile, with Tata's tales of Beirut's war and Mama's dreams of return, she offered me stories of resistance, of rootedness and presence on the land. Her face would light up every time she talked about the First Intifada, how her daughters were out on the front line. "They would come running down the street as soon as the Israelis started firing, alongside kids I've never seen before, and I would usher them into the house—under the bed and in the closet." Once, a teenager with a keffiyeh wrapped around his face darted into the house. She told him to whip it off and sit at the kitchen table. Israeli soldiers barged in just as she was serving him food. "He's my grandson," she told them when they claimed he was hurtling rocks at tanks. "He's been here eating the whole time. Get out of my house." She giggled to me, "But of course he's my grandson, just like you are. You're all my children here." She saw herself as a Tata of the revolution, another one of our maternal giants nourishing and sustaining our struggle. She spoke of the Israeli army with a passion that, like my Tata's, was full of dignity. "We know where we're from," she would say. "Only the settlers are confused about their identity, claiming a homeland that is not theirs."

Fed spiritually and physically, I set about fixing the flat she let out, which had no heating, no internet, and no phone connection. Ramallah's stone houses could never warm up the way our homes in Amman do, and I resigned myself to cold showers as I shivered my way through the first few weeks of arrival. Slowly, I learned how to exist under Israeli apartheid, where the politics of visibility and invisibility mark the difference between life and death. Which checkpoints to cross when, how to move in Israeli-controlled Palestinian cities like Haifa and Akka, how to interact with regime enforcers. The darting shadows had me well trained to pass unnoticed, and I spent my days roaming the breadth of Palestine, from its River Jordan to its Mediterranean Sea. In the evenings, I retreated to the balcony of Aida's flat where, one day, a lover planted a jasmine bush for me in a clay pot, in a spot that we had agreed most suited it: the corner closest to my office window, overlooking the valley below and Mahmoud Darwish's tomb on the other side. I had not seen the flat before renting it, but like all coincidences during my time in Palestine, from meeting Aida onward, that choice—with its homage to Darwish—seemed preordained. Not least because the spectacular view reminded me of al-Abdali.

There on my balcony, I sat, hour after hour, cigarette after cigarette, writing, rewriting. Losing myself. *Finding myself*, my mind mutters. Little by little, under the ghastliest of circumstances, this space suspended over the hills of Ramallah became a place of magic, as I got radicalized in the most glorious sense. Palestine, a bubble of beauty enmeshed in ugliness, is covered and covering. And she held my hand as I wrote through the lies of my life, shedding all the layers and tossing all the masks, jotting down all the words that remain unsaid, uncovering, embracing my abject self.

◆ ◆ ◆

I write to Ramzi, that figment of my imagination. The little boy sitting next to me in Amman's alleyways who has become the illusory man to whom I confess my thoughts and against whom I find myself. I share with him, and with that quiet boy who sat next to him night after night without saying much. I tell them what my return to Palestine teaches me: that our present is not our own, that our lives begin long before we are born. I tell them that I now see there is fire within me, too. That I did, with time, grow up to be the fighter Baba had wanted me to be. First, Palestine had to teach me what is worth fighting for. Teach me, also, what being a man means, ending my failed effort to emulate the only vision of manhood I had foolishly thought worthy. Where I felt banished before, this land has brought me back to my people, where I belong, and for whom I fight.

As I begin writing this to Ramzi, making sense of the lives and decades between our final conversation and this letter, an anger that has long been held back overwhelms me, makes me want to break bones and draw blood. At first, this pain latches on to Ramzi, our story and the love we had for each other. But I swiftly move past that and see this anger as one that speaks of injustices inflicted over countless days, spanning generations, passed from womb to child, and made more acute with each beginning. Calamities that seep into our skin and become part of our lives, never confronted, never transitioning into history.

From my balcony here, looking out at Darwish's shrine month after month, I see Palestinians in Gaza singing, walking, dancing their way to the fence I crossed, seeking nothing more than dignity and justice, to return to their homes. Israeli soldiers hiding behind sand dunes—cowardly and camouflaged and decked out with the deadliest technology—snipe them off, one at a time, for no reason other than that they can, frightened by a Palestinian asserting their presence. And supposedly civilized nations hail Israel's accomplishments, moronically parroting Zionist rhetoric, pretending that Israel is facing hordes of terrorists. A catchall descriptor that erases our history and justifies all forms of evil to be unleashed against us. For that is all we are in their eyes. It is all we have ever been. It is a farce that colonialism can replay itself, over and over.

It is our failing that we have not learned. Our colonizers have always colonized. That is what they do, and we are nothing but dispensable bodies for their white war machines. But as our brothers and sisters get killed in Gaza, our supposed leaders, in Ramallah and beyond, say nothing. They imprison, torture, and murder anyone who does. What new lows have we sunk to?

I finally have the words to respond to Ramzi, to his childish diatribes about our people. We *are* the downtrodden of the world, I want to agree with him. Our people have become unthinking, uncritical. Holding on to the very little that gives their lives meaning: gods that offer no justification for our current misery, kings and presidents who have done nothing to deserve their thrones. And instead of asking why, and what can be done about it, we sink into a perpetual cycle of self-defeat and cynicism or else distract ourselves with shiny objects and nauseating wealth. We are the people who get stomped on by greater nations today. We are pillaged and raped and our spineless rulers grovel for more. We are collectively living in the delusion of a past greatness, one that has made way for a crippling malaise. We put down our weakest to disguise our hollowness. We tread on the most vulnerable to show strength. We police our lives to deflect from our paralysis.

Whatever pride our ancestors might have had has given way to shame, to defeat. It is not only our colonizers we must confront; it is the gaze of our own we must hold.

The questions I should have asked Ramzi in those alleyways in Amman:

What kind of Haifa would my grandparents have built had our armies stood their ground and prevented their expulsion? What heights would Beirut have reached had its supposed leaders not destroyed it with their own hands? What future would Mama have had if her survival was not made contingent on acquiescence? What life could we, you and I, have enjoyed, had I not been ostracized?

When did we become so small that these questions feel immense?

I know what he would answer: *What does all this have to do with me?*

Everything. It has everything to do with you, and with me. Our pessimism is so deep, so entrenched and unfathomable, that we cannot begin to take responsibility for it. Our glorious revolutions of this past decade have been crushed. Our people in Gaza are being annihilated. Gargantuan efforts are needed to demand something as basic as dignity, as millions of brave souls take to the street, shouting for lives worth living, only to be shot down and killed, imprisoned, condemned to a life where dignity is an unimaginable luxury. The pain is too big for us to hold. It is easier to retreat, to saddle our high horses and pretend we are better than everyone around us. Isn't that what you and I did in our nightly meanders? Looked out and judged Amman and everyone within it? We and people around us drive ourselves into a frenzy of policing morals, imposing religion on ourselves and our kids, upholding social expectations and 3eib. For what? What has our apathy done to us? Where has our acquiescence taken us?

A familiar bitterness rises in the back of my throat, prompting me, finally, to tell you what I should have said that day two decades ago, when you last called me. After spending countless hours listening to you complain about everything, decry the backwardness of others around us—suddenly, you turn on me? I should have told you and your parents to fuck right off. When it came down to it, your liberal proclamations were nothing but a useful facade to cover up the fact that you were hiding behind the same shroud of propriety that you mocked others for upholding. Banishing me from your home for fear of, what, contagion, or scandal, or divine retribution? Fuck you for making me a fair price to pay to keep your family's appearance of civility and to protect its honor—that bastard concept that censors our humanity. Fuck this notion of morality when it demonizes and destroys its own. And fuck you for accepting that I was unwelcome among my own people.

Ramzi, we are all complicit in maintaining the suffocating norms that shackle our communities. No one is going to save us—we must do the work ourselves. We are all playing our part upholding the tyranny ruling over us even as we protest it. Pitiful we have become, when my Palestinian words are privileged next to the words of Syrians or Yemenis, Libyans or Sudanese. You think me delusional, drawing connections between our tale and the waves of history. Or too Westernized. Maybe it is the definition of vanity to relate my personal emancipation to that of the region. But you see, here, too, a continuum exists—between your silence and our collective oppression. It is in the most intimate of whispers that revolutions will be born. It is in the space between the two of us that we should have fought harder. We must each undo our own binds, break through the narratives that colonizers and dictators impose on us to make us feel smaller, to turn us into perpetual victims, to condemn us to a life of shame.

This is not a fitting outburst. I must apologize. My anger sometimes fills me with a power that feels invincible, as if I could harness all this injustice, link arms with the millions who are putting their bodies on the front line to fight for a future full of justice and tolerance and humanity. Our region is heaving with the desire for a new language. Bursting at the seams to birth an alternate future. Even though we have descended into a hell that confirms our wildest nightmares, with Gaza facing genocidal violence that is unbridled, there is no going back to those days when we accepted the blinders put over our eyes. We are in the throes of a rebirth. And yet, often, the resignation of those around me leaves me feeling broken, alone, as I lie powerlessly enraged in the face of inertia.

50

AFTER two years of living in Palestine, my invisibility falters and my permits are refused. Another generation, another expulsion. It happened smoothly, like someone locking the front door the minute I stepped out for an errand. Criminals often work in the cover of night.

I land back in London, and Aida and I migrate our conversations to the phone. Incredibly, she waits for my return, leaving the flat vacant. Hers is the steadfastness against Israeli oppression that comes naturally to the generation that lived through the Nakba. A year after my forced departure, she calls me, sounding bashful. She could not wait for my return any longer; the flat had to be let out. There is a German lady who is interested, but she will ask her to leave the minute the Israelis allow me to reenter. "You are my grandson, you are family now," she whispers in a conspiratorial tone. My own generation's cynicism means that I have succumbed much sooner, knowing full well that the Israelis will drag their feet before they allow me to return. I have already sent a friend to pack up my belongings. I tell Aida as much, to ease her guilt, and promise to keep trying to return.

VII

51

THE news reaches me that Ramzi's first child has been born. A baby boy. He has waited a long time for this moment. Imagined it a lifetime ago when we roamed Amman's alleyways. Fatherhood will suit him, of this there is no doubt. The little one is lucky to have landed in his arms, even at this moment on our convulsing, virus-ridden planet. His pride is emanating all the way from the Gulf to my doorstep here in London, where my heart is reveling.

Reveling and breaking open once more. I imagine him holding his boy in his arms and think to myself, *We have work to do, to make our region somewhere he can live with the dignity he deserves.* Our childhoods, his and mine, taught us to fear such dreams. Fantasies of a better world are dangerous. Instead of dignity, we were raised on dread, of saying or doing the wrong thing. We were taught to flee. Those who remain are retreating into their homes and families, shrinking their dreams. To remain, too, can be a form of flight.

❖ ❖ ❖

On one of my visits to the Gulf, I imagine asking Ramzi if he would like to meet, to go for a drink. In my daydreams, Ramzi is standing in a high-rise glass building, after a long day's work, looking out into the mist coming in from the sea. His wife, whom I have never met, is in the kitchen; the smell of her cooking fills his apartment. There is music playing in the background—classical tunes or some soft Arabic ballad. Next to him, a whiskey tumbler with two ice cubes rests on a Palestinian-embroidered coaster, one from a set his wife bought to support refugees in Jordanian camps. I knock on his door, or call him, or send a WhatsApp message. The form my intrusion takes is less important than his response. I try to guess the very first thought to surface in his mind when he hears from me. Wish for a way to capture that uncensored reaction, to see how different it is from my own recollections of us.

He agrees. I see us sitting at a place of his choice. This is his city, not mine. He chooses somewhere quiet, a patio by the water. It is warm and we both want to sit outside. The Gulf's musky night makes me nostalgic for a second, and brave enough to contemplate moving back home. I quickly dismiss this thought. We settle in our seats on the outer edge of the seating area. Behind us is a table of older men, smoking cigars, drinking. I turn to Ramzi, study his face, an echo from my past. A belly where there was none before presses against the front of his white shirt. Instead of a scalp, he has thick black hair, gelled backward. He looks older, tired, but there is the same warmth in his gray eyes. His small hands are on the table, fumbling with his lighter.

I am impatient and speak first. "Is this place a regular of yours?" I ask. "No," he says, "it is far from home." I understand. No one will see us here. I do not initiate other questions and fall back into past, forgotten habits, leaving it to him to take the lead. He is anxious to get the waiter's attention, and when he does, he orders his whiskey, with two ice cubes, and pulls out his packet of Marlboro Reds. "Can I have one?" I ask. He looks at me, raises an eyebrow, pushes the packet toward me. I half expect him to flash me his mischievous grin. *Oh, now you want one?* He doesn't. That grin, which I so cherished, is reserved for closer drinking companions, not strangers or acquaintances. That is all I have become.

Its absence, and the pang in my chest, remind me how far we've parted, how little of his time I can command. As if to drive the point home, he shoots me an impatient glance, one that lets me know I am on borrowed time. He wants to get this over and done with. I realize with rising horror that he has only agreed to a meeting to avoid being rude. At most, he wants to lay to rest a faint curiosity about how things have turned out. He has no interest in a long-overdue conversation. We are not thirteen anymore, or fifteen, or seventeen, or whenever it was that he last cherished our intimacies. Enough time has passed.

I become nervous, regretting having called him and wanting not to burden him with my presence anymore. Nor with the unsettling realization that reveals itself. The one I tell myself I will grapple with later even as I neutralize it on the spot, knowing I will not return to it in the future. The whisper that tells me I have long been missing him. Missing his eyes, fixed on me again, and his hands, twirling his cigarette packet on the table between us. I resist the urge to reach out and hold them, to look them over, to inspect any changes they may have accrued along the way. There will be no hand holding. I have been well trained in his presence. There is no room for such inappropriate behavior where we are sitting.

Closure, I think to myself, is best left transactional. There is no longer a need to fear what I am about to say, given that it has been said to him already, by others, by time. I take a deep breath and tell him what he already knows. "I am gay," I say. Three words that distill years of confusion. I am struck by how innocuous they sound. Words that I haven't considered telling him before, in the heat of it all, put off as I was by their foreignness, by what I thought was their vileness. Encouraged by how easily they fit, I go further. I am no longer fearful of losing him, or of seeing disgust in his eyes. I recount that I am married to a brilliant and adoring husband, we have a beautiful home in London, and we're getting a dog. A swift tumble of an update—one dripping with domesticity.

As soon as the rush of words jumps out of my mouth, I realize that none of these disclosures are what I have come to unveil. I look at him, await his reaction. I half expect him to down his whiskey and stand up, resentful for my bringing this back into his life. *It is undignified*, he might say, *especially here*. Our cities are sheltered from the improprieties that people have unashamedly embraced elsewhere. There is no justifiable reason for someone to parade their immorality with such confidence, or to assume that their comfort with depravity, cultivated in places like London, can be brought back home. He is irritated by what must have become a long-forgotten nuisance. I am certain he still rails against everything while safely ensconced in his tower. He does not have to deal with any of this unappealing behavior in his day-to-day, I imagine. He is naturally unaware, living in his high-rise, that under his feet, the Gulf has fashioned a gay underground that rivals the wildest in London.

He says nothing, but I see his eyes darting to the table of men behind us. Again, I understand. "Go," I tell him as soon as I read that impulse in his eyes. "Don't worry. Your departure will not wreck me again. I will finish my drink and take a stroll outside." I try to make that *Go* as light as possible, to hide the fact that it is pregnant with all that would be left hanging between us if he really did leave. Regret that I have placed myself at his mercy again. Self-consciousness that my being could warrant such repugnance from someone I once loved, from someone who once loved me. Affirmation that I have done the right thing by shutting him out all those years ago. An unending sadness at our smallness as men.

He does not leave. He purses his lips, as he used to do when he was thinking, or serious, or slightly uncomfortable. Another cigarette is pulled out of the packet. I feel braver, hopeful that there might be a kernel of affection for me left within him. Oddly, I am grateful that he is not repulsed by me, or at least not sufficiently repulsed to leave. The threshold for what I deem insulting inexplicably rises when I am back home. I slowly make my way to the one disclosure that matters. "I wonder," I say, "if you ever realized how deeply I loved you. I myself did not until years after we parted. For the longest time, you remained the only man I loved."

My mind conjures this reunion. But I know that if I were ever to sit opposite him again, studying his features, words—Arabic or English—would fail me. And in any case, we have both moved on. There is no need to add to his weariness, to the exhaustion we all carry in our bones these days. My memory of him is beloved, and the closest I will venture toward ever seeing him again is to keep driving by his house on the way to mine whenever I am back in Amman. Homage to an old habit.

That is why, as I draft these final words, on a short trip to the Gulf, where I am staying a mere few meters from his home, I refrain from calling. I write this instead, with no expectation or recrimination. This is a cowardly act, a passive one, in keeping with my side of our history. Sometimes I doubt my intentions. In the unforgiving light of adulthood, our story is nothing more than a childhood crush. Why, then, have I dwelled on this for more than two decades?

A few years later, Ramzi's sister called me. She had heard from Maya that we both happened to be in Amman. She asked if we could meet for coffee. I hesitated. He—and by extension his sister—had become precious figments of my imagination. There is no world in which we could reclaim what was lost, and there was no use in trying. But in abstract form, he had given me much to think about, and I owed him a great deal for that. I was still protective of him, of us, in this illusory reality. Begrudgingly, I accepted the invitation. I sat opposite her in Books@Café, studying features that faintly reminded me of a kid I once knew. She had been a young teenager when I last saw her, she was now a mother. Although much was different, an intense familiarity reasserted itself. The way she looked at me with a cheeky smile. How her eyes glanced self-consciously to the side when she made a remark that she thought funny. Her effort to dispel the awkwardness between us was endearing. Her eyes, a greener version of his, were difficult to hold.

She arrived as harried as young mothers often are, aware that the time she had carved out could be interrupted at any moment by a child's request, more pressing than any matter she sought to attend to. It took her very little time to steer us to the place she needed. Minutes after we sat down—minutes that were filled with an unwelcome politeness where once there was intimacy—she apologized. "I did not know what had happened for years," she blurted. Suddenly, I had gone from being a sibling of sorts to hovering like an invisible presence in their home. There was never an explanation offered, from Ramzi, or their parents. Only that I would not be visiting anymore, and consequently, that there was no need for me to be mentioned. "It was as if you had been placed behind a wall." She regrets not asking for details or pressing for an explanation. But the ferocity of their reaction, of her parents' determination, of Ramzi's withdrawal, made any interrogation impossible. "I still should have tried," she repeated. A hand extended, she wanted me to know, signaled to me discreetly, that she had no problem with gay people.

There was very little to say in response. I regurgitated the things I had done, some of the places I had been to since we had last seen each other. We both made a cursory effort to package the events of two decades into a narrative that might make sense, or at least suggest we had chosen the lives that had unfurled before us. Hers as a chef. Mine as a writer. Beneath the layers of that conversation, just below the surface, Ramzi was—as always—present. Yet neither of us spoke about him. For once, it was he who was made absent.

52

AS I finally place Ramzi's correspondence back into the yellow box and clear out my desk, it dawns on me that I have been writing this for seventeen years, in spurts here and there, leaving tatters in journals and loose papers, ready to be compiled. But I had been unable to complete it until I mastered a skill learned elsewhere: to put distance between the writer and subject. A necessary skill to grapple with his world, the one I could never let go of, but which let go of me. In that space I came to inhabit, a great guilt arose: I was the one who had left. I had let him down. Deceived him, betrayed our commitment that our friendship would last a lifetime. With that acquired distance, I was able to see more clearly what had transpired in the days and months after our call. It dawned on me that perhaps I, the writer of the letter, was in truth the arsonist who burned the whole thing down.

I realize, too, that in writing this book, I am, at least in part, re-creating—perhaps reliving—that last letter I had sent him, offering once more a grotesque revelation of truths that are too ugly to be uttered in our milieu. An arsonist on a burning binge. *Will this text get me banished again?* This time, it hardly matters. I don't quite know how to be anything other than banished, living on the outside, in shadows, in queer spaces, between worlds. Even this most personal of texts I write in a language that is not my own, a foreign tongue that has become a reliable one, without yet dispelling its foreignness. In taking it on, I failed to scrub this adopted language of its violence, its arrogance. Yet reclaiming my Arabic is a fraught endeavor, like visiting the site of an unpleasant memory. The association is visceral. Embodying that language puts me in the shoes of the kid who was hated, or rather, who hated himself. I remain bereft, at home neither here nor there.

If Ramzi ever reads this, he will open it in a world immersed in Arabic. Those around him will say I have become Western, speaking in their language, cherishing their values. Others around me will condemn Ramzi's backwardness, his conservatism. If only things were that simple; we are, both he and I, here and there, us and them. Even as we build worlds apart, one immersed in English, the other in Arabic, we are figuring out the limits of what binds us together. Neither language makes either of us whole.

53

EVERY night, my husband's hairy chest tickles my back. He bends his knees, spooning mine, propping me like a pillow. His arm falls across my body and I contort to fit myself into the space beneath it. He begins snoring softly before I have even settled in, his warm breath on the back of my neck. Lying in the dark, I think to myself: *This is one of my favorite places to be.* This is home. "Look after each other," Baba had said to him soon after they met. He, too, could see that I had found my home. This place that I love. Sometimes, I wake up hours later, hot and sweaty, and I disentangle myself from his embrace. Come up for air. He turns away from me, barely missing a beat in his breath. Other times, I crawl out of my beloved cave much sooner. I stretch myself next to him, facing him, wondering if his body is saddened when I put space between us.

◆ ◆ ◆

We were at a friend's wedding in the south of Spain and my phone was ringing. The ceremony had just ended and rounds of loud ululations from the bride's younger cousins, the contingent that had flown in from Palestine, were rattling through the air. The bride and groom, glowing in the light of the sun dipping into the Mediterranean, were standing under a makeshift altar of lemons and oranges held together by rosemary and olive branches. Guests had begun scattering, and my husband had gone to grab us some champagne. I hung around, watching them, feeling a great deal of joy mingled with some nostalgia for their certainty and innocence, both of which had matured in my then decade-long relationship. *Baba* flashed on my screen. My husband and I had just left him and Mama in Beirut a few days prior, where they had settled after Baba's retirement.

"I'm just having a glass of your favorite wine by the sea next to Mama, and we were talking about you. I wanted to call to tell you that we miss you. When are you coming to visit us?"

"Baba, we literally just left you."

"I know, I know. But I want you both to move here so we can see you all the time."

"OK, Baba, maybe one day," I chuckled.

"Tareq?"

"Yes?"

"I'm proud of you."

I hung up before he could hear the lump in my throat. It had been a long path to these four words. Gentle nudges and patient work had moved him from his fear to a place of love—sedatives were no longer needed to calm his anxieties.

The wedding party began posing for pictures and I wandered away. My friend had gushed about the groom flying in a ham cutter from his village in northern Spain and I made my way over to eye the spread. I grabbed a couple of slices, mumbling my *gracias* to the expert carver hunched over a leg of ham, and turned to scan the guests. That's when his eyes locked on mine. A handsome young man from the bride's party, standing alone. He held my gaze intensely, a full-on stare that lasted long enough to dissolve the initial feeling of flattery. طنط خول! My heartbeat quickened as insults from my school days careened into my head. The beating sun, the salty air, and the snippets of Arabic conversation in the background transported me to Amman, and I was again in the school courtyard. Dressed in my finest and standing on our own stretch of the Spanish coast, I found myself looking into the eyes of Mustapha Aboud from twenty years ago, frozen.

I broke the man's stare and latched on to an acquaintance passing by, thankful for the distraction. The rest of the evening flowed seamlessly, and by the end of dinner, we were all given espadrilles to slip onto our feet as guests hit the dance floor. My husband and I walked around the beach and I mentioned that there was a man leering at me, but he didn't seem too concerned. "Oh, he's hot," he cooed when I pointed him out. Anxiety clawed at me. I was ashamed that I might have been too open, *too gay*, in this space. *Had I offended this man? Was I inappropriate in this setting?* I surveyed the dance floor and noncommittally swayed on the outer ring. Time and again, my eyes found his, and I tried brushing it off, increasingly annoyed by this intrusion. The full moon threw its rays over the crowd dancing to Spanish and Arabic beats. After a few glasses of champagne, the edge wore off and, impulsively, I made my way over to where the staring man was swaying.

"Hi," I said, extending my hand, "I don't think we've had a chance to meet."

He turned to me. His eyes were green like mine, and much less menacing up close. He was young. Much younger than I had initially thought when we stared each other down across the beach. It made sense why I would remember my high school bullies; he was barely out of high school himself. Extending his hand to meet mine, he gave me an unsure smile and it dawned on me: the bullies in my head were my own demons; this man wanted nothing more than a casual hookup further along the beach.

"I'm Ala'a," he said.

"Wonderful to meet you. I'm Tareq."

His pupils glazed over in confusion.

"Derek?" he asked.

"No, no, it's Tareq," I said again, pronouncing my name as I would in Arabic.

"Oh."

Apprehension filled his face. He did not need to offer an explanation. *He thought me foreign, not someone from the bride's party, someone who might know his family.* Still holding his hand, and wishing to rid us both of our demons, I pulled him onto the dance floor.

54

EACH time I return to Amman, I sit next to Tata. Hold her hands in my own and tell her of Palestine. She is tiny and old, tired, wrapped in woolen shawls, blind, and toothless. She tells me she is bored of waiting for her God to invite her up. "It is time. It has been time for years. It is time that I see your Jiddo again." Her bony hands rest in mine and she tilts her ear toward me. She rubs her fingers against each other. "To warm their tips," she says, as she anxiously distracts herself from the memories flooding in. Wisps of white hair catch the light as I recount tales of my return. Of having found the house she had fled from in Haifa, when she was a young seventeen-year-old full of sight. Of how I located the house based solely on her description of how to reach it from the city's main boulevard at the foot of the mountain. Of having smelled the jasmine in that entrance, the same fragrance she took in on the night of her dispossession. Of having stood in front of her school—which is now a museum—weeping, unable to walk in.

Tata says nothing. She does not interrupt. I share a memory, wait, worry. *Am I overwhelming her? Is it cruel to bring this up, or cathartic?* She looks into the distance, unseeing, her eyes fixated on the muted TV playing, as always, Christian sermons. Her hand motionless in mine. When I stop, she turns to me, never rushing me. She, too, is worried, about my presence in Palestine, about my inability to let go. I collect myself and carry on. It is only when I tell her about the school that she stops me. "The one at the top of the hill," she asks, "you found it?" I answer that I did. "Accidentally," I say. "I was passing by, and there was a plaque on the wall of a museum. I stood to read the plaque and discovered it had been a school—*your* school." She falls silent again. Neither of us says anything else for a minute or two. She sighs. "What do I know?" she says. "What do I know what all this is for? The answer sits with our Lord. He works in mysterious ways."

My chest constricts. I sit with her some more, tell her about the school. The buildings around it. How long it took me to walk from there to her house. How impressed I was that she did that walk every day on her own as a child. I do not tell her that my husband was standing next to me when I accidentally stumbled upon it. One strand of my story makes Tata proud. The other would not. She is the only one in my family who does not know I am married. I hide it—not in shame, I tell myself, but out of respect. I do not know how to hold myself whole under her gaze. That is OK. Much of my life has taught me how to make parts of myself invisible to suit those I love. Mine is a truth that is absent from her world, and it is far too late to introduce it. Not that it matters; her love is felt deeply, I know, and that must suffice for now.

Instead, we stay with Palestine. Behind her closed eyelids, she imagines returning, reclaiming a stolen past, knowing she never will. Her God will soon heed her plea and invite her to His side. I, too, conjure images of an alternative utopia to the world we are both sitting in. Unlike Tata, my destination is not a reconciled past but an imagined future where none of us must cover, or absent, a part of ourselves to live.

ACKNOWLEDGMENTS

THIS book is an echo of an experience, perhaps more accurately describing a life as it is remembered than as it was lived. There are necessary alterations and omissions, the messiness of fitting complex experiences into a neat narrative arc. Some scenes and individual characteristics have been lightly fictionalized to protect the privacy of those involved. All resulting errors—and I am sure there are a few—are entirely my own.

I have been writing this since 2006—in notes scribbled here and there. This exercise might not have culminated in this book were it not for Bill Clegg. Bill: Sometimes I think you are a dream my mind conjured to keep me going. Thank you for showing me what being an ally means, for your friendship, and for fighting in my corner. There is so much to fight—but with you, it all seems possible somehow. My gratitude extends to everyone at the Clegg Agency. Marion Duvert: for your endless support and embrace of any challenge I bring your way. Simon Toop: for the thoughtful and seemingly effortless way you keep everything running so smoothly.

Jenny Xu: for advocating for this book from the minute it landed on your desk. I am in awe of your spirit, your diligence and sensitivity, and the great editorial skill you brought to bear on this text. Ansa Khan Khattak: Your attention to detail, the care and commitment with which you approached each line—it was a thrill having your editorial contributions. Every interaction with the teams at both Washington Square Press and Sceptre has been a joy. A special shout-out to Holly Rice, Maudee Genao, and Ifeoma Anyoku. I am so comforted to have you as the midwives for this book's journey into the world. Shelby Pumphrey, Lloyd Davis, Kelli McAdams: for your care and support. For the beautiful cover art, Rana Samara.

Earlier pieces of this book appeared in various publications.

"Dreams of a Palestine Where I Can Hold Myself Whole" in *Skin Deep*, and "The Loss of Tatas" in *The Baffler*. The segment on Gaza appeared in a more expanded version in an anthology of essays titled *Their Borders, Our World: Building New Solidarities with Palestine*, published by Haymarket Books. Mahdi Sabbagh: for including me in this prescient volume. PalFest: for fighting to make room for our voices. An excerpt, "Confronting the Abject: What Gaza Can Teach Us About the Struggles That Shape Our World," appeared in *LitHub*.

After a dreamy cigarette on my balcony in Ramallah, a journey began to transport an excerpt of this book onto the big screen. Caitlin McLeod and Jessica Palmarozza: for turning my words into stunning visuals in *One Like Him*. The film crew and actors in Palestine and Jordan: Working with you was a highlight of my writing years.

Countless works accompanied me on this journey, but there are specific citations that need to be acknowledged. The "continuum" from Rebecca Solnit's *Recollections of My Nonexistence*; the "Arab malaise" from Samir Kassir's *Being Arab*; a "life worth living" from Mahmoud Darwish's poem "We Have on This Earth What Makes Life Worth Living"; "Jewish strangers" from Raja Shehadeh's *Strangers in the House: Coming of Age in Occupied Palestine*; "covering" from Kenji Yoshino's *Covering: The Hidden Assault on Our Civil Rights*; the "abject" from Julia Kristeva's *Powers of Horror*; and the painfully apt description of being "powerlessly enraged" from Lina Mounzer's essay "Letter from Beirut: From Revolution to Pandemic."

Many people left their imprints on these pages, from the earliest drafts to the final iterations. For your reactions, insights, and critical interventions: Jill, Saleem, Naomi, Mona, Catherine, Hana, Miguel, Zena, Safwan, Marian. Yara: for reading and before that for giving me a home in Palestine. Isabella: for your generous instruction, but, more than that, for your friendship. Blue Mountain Center Residency: for holding the space.

It took me a long time to understand that writing is not a task to be done but a life to be lived. So much life happened as I was writing this book. Looking through these completed pages, I can now see I was trying to immortalize all those who were being taken away before

I was ready. I could never be ready. Professor Joffé: Your fierce intelligence and endless patience were gifts. I am grateful for your mentorship. Khalo: Your stories colored my childhood. I miss them. Tata Marcel: I hope you found peace. We are indebted to you for holding down the fort in Beirut for all these years. Tata Eva: I miss you all day, every day, and see you in every bird that crosses my path.

Baba: I was in the middle of a conversation with you. I wish you had given me just a little more time. But then, you had already given me so much, and no time would have ever been enough. I am left with an ocean of love and a grief colossus.

الله يرحمكم

This personal anguish is dwarfed and is itself a luxury next to the death and devastation we are all witnessing. As I write these words, Israel's genocide against Palestinians grinds on, sadistic and incomprehensible. The loss is staggering, and the futility of narrative in the face of such violence is devastating. Our world has been cleaved open, and there are no words that might make sense of this rupture, or of the rock-solid conviction that many of us carry within our hearts, that there will be justice one day, and Palestine will be free.

الله يرحم الشهداء ويصبر اهلهم

Mama, brothers: I know you sometimes wonder about my choices, and don't quite understand why I do what I do. And yet, I have never felt abandoned, unsupported, or unloved. Thank you for never introducing conditionality into our family. Mama: You have blazed a trail that I am lucky to have inherited. Fear not, the struggle continues.

Seth: None of this would have been possible without you, my witness, my home.

ABOUT THE AUTHOR

TAREQ BACONI is a Palestinian writer, scholar, and activist. He is the grandson of refugees from Jerusalem and Haifa and grew up between Amman and Beirut. His work has appeared in, among others, *The New York Times* and *The Baffler*, and he contributes essays to *The New York Review of Books* and the *London Review of Books*. He has also written for film; his award-winning BFI short *One Like Him*, a queer love story set in Jordan, was screened at over thirty festivals. He is also the author of *Hamas Contained: A History of Palestinian Resistance*, which was shortlisted for the Palestine Book Award.

WASHINGTON SQUARE PRESS, an imprint of Simon & Schuster, fosters an open environment where ideas flourish, bestselling authors soar to new heights, and tomorrow's finest voices are discovered and nurtured. Since its launch in 2002, Atria has published hundreds of bestsellers and extraordinary books, which would not have been possible without the invaluable support and expertise of its team and publishing partners. Thank you to the Atria Books colleagues who collaborated on *Fire in Every Direction*, as well as to the hundreds of professionals in the Simon & Schuster advertising, audio, communications, design, ebook, finance, human resources, legal, marketing, operations, production, sales, supply chain, subsidiary rights, and warehouse departments who help Atria bring great books to light.

EDITORIAL
Jenny Xu
Ifeoma Anyoku

JACKET DESIGN
Kelli McAdams
Rana Samara

MARKETING
Maudee Genao

MANAGING EDITORIAL
Paige Lytle
Shelby Pumphrey
Lacee Burr
Sofia Echeverry

PRODUCTION
Kathleen Rizzo
Chloe Gray
Lloyd Davis
Esther Paradelo
Ritika Karnik

PUBLICITY
Holly Rice

PUBLISHING OFFICE
Dana Trocker
Abby Velasco

SUBSIDIARY RIGHTS
Nicole Bond
Sara Bowne
Rebecca Justiniano